D1029206

Dress in France in the Eighteenth Century

Dress in France in the Eighteenth Century

Madeleine Delpierre

Translated by Caroline Beamish

Yale University Press
New Haven and London

Designed by Laura Church
Printed in Hong Kong

Library of Congress Cataloging-in-Publication Data

Delpierre, Madeleine. 1920–1994
Dress in France in the Eighteenth Century / Madeleine Delpierre
p. cm.
Includes bibliographical references and index.
ISBN 0-300-07128-0 (cloth: alk. paper)
1. Costume–France–History–18th century.
2. France–Social life and customs.
3. France–History–18th century.
I. Title.

GT860.D43 1997
391' .00944' 09034–dc21 97–26412
CIP

A catalogue record for this book is available from
The British Library

CONTENTS

Foreword

Madeleine Delpierre (1920–1994)

This book was written during the last years of Madeleine Delpierre's life, when she was in daily contact with historical costumes, particularly costumes of the eighteenth century, which she liked best.

She started working in the Musée Carnavalet in 1947, under the guidance of François Boucher and then of Jacques Wilhem; she took over curatorship of the costumes donated to the Ville de Paris in 1920 by the Société de l'Histoire du Costume, founded in 1907 by the painters Maurice Leloir and Edouard Detaille. The first exhibition she was involved in was the exhibition of French eighteenth-century costume in 1954; the last was 'Modes et Révolutions en 1989'.

Thanks to Madeleine Delpierre, the Musée de la Mode et du Costume, an annexe of the Musée Carnavalet, became an independent museum and was housed from 1977 in the Palais Galliera. During the forty years she spent there, the museum was host to a great variety of exhibitions; she attracted many gifts and was responsible for numerous purchases, with the result that the museum now contains one of the most important collections of costume in the world, a life's work, as she herself used to say. Finishing the work that Maurice Leloir, another tireless worker who also loved the eighteenth century, had begun forty years earlier, she established herself as one of the pioneers of costume history, along with celebrated names like Quicherat, Lacroix and Franklin.

Illness prevented her from putting the final touches to this book and bringing the bibliography up to date. I hope with these few words to express the gratitude of the museum, of which she was the first creator, of the Société de l'Histoire du Costume, of which she was treasurer, and of the international committee of ICOM, of which she was one of the first members.

Françoise Tétart-Vittu

Preface

In this book the history of French costume is considered from a social, economic and literary point of view, as well as from an aesthetic one, at a period when, sustained by the cultural prestige of Versailles, French dress achieved an extraordinary level of elegance and was the focal point of rich and distinguished society in Europe. Men and women of fashion in the eighteenth century either acquired clothing directly from the great Parisian retailers or imitated their wares, sometimes adapting them to suit local tradition.

The book opens with a study of the development of French fashion, for women, men and children, between 1718, the date at which the 'panier' – the single most important item of female clothing in the eighteenth century – made its first appearance in France, and 1795, when the female body, finally liberated from all accessories designed to shape or mould it, recovered its natural form and suppleness. The second part traces the development of the principal garments, of underwear and of accessories (those worn on the body such as frills and furbelows, caps and hats, gloves and muffs, stockings and shoes; and those carried in the hand such as bags and purses, fans and handkerchiefs, parasols, umbrellas and canes). The materials from which clothes were made (fabrics and lace that perfectly reflected the artistic trends of the time) are also discussed.

The second part concludes with a consideration of the comparisons that can be made with fashions from abroad (England, the Holy Roman Empire, the Low Countries, Switzerland and the Scandinavian countries, as well as the Latin countries – Spain, Portugal, Italy – and, finally, the countries of Eastern Europe – Russia and Poland). It is shown that although formal or ceremonial dress, inevitably part of long, local traditions, was little influenced by French taste, the fashionable clothing of elegant society was affected far beyond the confines of the kingdom of France.

Part three contains information on the clothes worn for special occasions (baptism, first communion, marriage and mourning) and on ceremonial costume (the symbolic and semi-religious costume worn for coronations, the apparel of the orders of chivalry, ceremonial court dress, the clothes worn at formal balls and by guests at royal residences, ecclesiastical court dress, the full dress livery worn by royal pages, the uniforms of the king's guards and those worn by royal servants). The adornments of the cult of monarchy and the private wardrobes of the privileged classes are investigated, as well as the clothes of the working classes.

Part four is devoted to the professions and trades connected with clothing, their organisation (made more complex by the system of corporations) and their dispersal around Paris, the fashion capital of Europe. The cost of elegance is discussed (of which workers' pay constituted only a very small part) and also the dissemination of the latest fashions – assisted, before the appearance of fashion magazines at the end of the century, by the circulation of dolls and fashion plates.

Finally, in the last chapter, a number of works that throw light on the attitudes of contemporary writers to the costume of the time are examined. Novelists were fairly indifferent, whereas the authors of comedies, whose business it was to denounce excess, brought a more critical pen to the task; the memorialists, whose numbers began to multiply after the Revolution, wrote precisely, evocatively and often a little nostalgically about the late eighteenth century from their early nineteenth-century standpoint.

Introduction

In spite of some temporary excesses, exceptions perhaps that prove the rule, dress in eighteenth-century France achieved an extraordinary and sustained elegance. Thanks to the political, social, economic and cultural climate of the country, it became the inspiration for dress in the other countries of western Europe.

France was a monarchy, and the king (in the case of Louis XV, a good-looking and elegant man[1]) lived surrounded by a court that was originally the creation of Henri III but that had been considerably enlarged by Louis XIV. The court aimed to dazzle, and a good proportion of the income available to it was spent on ceremonial dress. The result might simply have been opulence and extravagance, but because of the influence of two women who successively held the sceptre of fashion, it instead became polished and elegant. Madame de Pompadour, the mistress of Louix XV (fig. 6), promoted a taste in dress that reflected the visual arts of the period, of which she was a keen supporter. Queen Marie-Antoinette, the consort of Louis XVI (fig. 14), was, as a very young woman, somewhat under the influence of her suppliers and in the early days of her reign lent her support to some extravagant styles, but later kept the whims of her designers under constant review. Neither of the two women, except possibly Marie-Antoinette on the eve of the Revolution, had any lasting influence on formal wear, which was more or less permanently tied to its heavy, traditional shapes. They did, on the other hand, affect current fashions by their readiness to try out ever more elegant and sometimes more comfortable alternatives.

The influence of Madame de Pompadour and Marie-Antoinette owed its strength to the fact that women in the eighteenth century, 'though having obtained no legal rights',[2] occupied a major position in society. Women were 'the governing principle, the guiding reason, the commanding voice [. . .]. Women kept the court in order and managed the home [. . .]. No catastrophe, no sweeping changes occurred that did not emanate from the action of women; the century was filled with female marvels, female excitements and adventures. Women's actions gave the period the twists and turns of a historical novel.'[3] Aristocratic and upper-class women were greatly admired; in their literary and philosophical salons, well-bred men practised good manners as though these were at the top of the list of cardinal virtues and allowed themselves to be swayed by women's opinions. The influence of women extended also to commerce and trade, to which they brought all their charm and sophistication. This explains why female costume began to exceed male dress in brilliance, men until now having always dressed more showily than women. Although on the verge of being submerged by the *esprit bourgeois*, which would turn it into a mere foil for women's dress, men's costume remained very elegant for a time, and often sported quite 'feminine' elements such as lace, embroidery and shimmering silks.

Society was not quite as segregated during this period as people tend to imagine. The aristocracy, some of whom were not at all wealthy, was bolstered by an influx of very wealthy financiers who bought their way into high society and tended to wear their clothes as a badge of their new social position. Marriages were contracted between these two classes, and the two worlds mingled, trying to outdo one another in elegance, to the great benefit of artisans and the luxury-goods industry.

All those involved in making clothes and accessories were based in Paris. By contrast, those who wore the clothes had, during the reign of Louis XIV, the Sun King, been obliged to reside in the king's new palace at Versailles. With the onset of the Regency in 1715, however, the whole court was hungry for freedom and pleasure; courtiers now spent only a quarter of the year at Versailles, during which time they discharged their duties to the monarch or the regent, and for the remaining months lived in Paris.

If the work of people involved in the creation of clothes (and because of the rules of the various corporations, these were numerous) was appreciated, that appreciation was owing to the very regulations imposed by the corporations. Although the rules regarding choice of fabric and working practices tended to curb originality, they guaranteed quality and enabled customers to buy with confidence. In some areas of production French craftsmen were still in need of the technical innovations and commercial relations with other countries that would allow them to carry out their craft to the highest standards. As far as silk manufacture was concerned, France had no reason to envy her neighbours; but the same was not true in relation to the importing and weaving of cotton, for which France still depended entirely on England. It was not until the end of the century that printed patterns on cotton (licensed only in 1760, in spite of strong demand and a considerable black market) began to be developed; after that, the light muslin dresses that were the harbingers of the fashions of the Directoire and the First Empire could be produced.

In spite of a decline in French political influence during the eighteenth century, the strength and attractiveness of French culture helped spread French fashion throughout Europe. The marriages made by the Bourbons, like the dispersal of the Huguenot craftsmen after the revocation of the Edict of Nantes in 1685, helped disseminate an influence that emanated to a large extent from the court at Versailles, which even the most minor courts in Europe emulated. Not only was French the international language of diplomacy, it was the language of a whole European élite. Moreover, French art set the tone for the liberal, active and progressive society that had developed to the west of the River Elbe. This delightful art, the rococo, had already begun to make its presence felt at the end of the reign of Louis XIV with a general softening of line in domestic decoration, and progressed smoothly from the curves of Louis-Quinze style to the straighter lines of Louis-Seize style. These styles were reflected in the cut of coats and dresses, and in the patterns of silks, with their sinuous garlands that developed gradually into shaded stripes. Costume and fabrics were the outward expression of a western civilisation in which the search for freedom of movement, for fantasy and pleasure 'refined taste and relaxed clothing'.[4]

Part One

Chapter One

Clothing and Fashion

The essence of fashion is its mutability. Without the caprices of fashion, clothing would never change, remaining as static as traditional costume, with the only variations being provided by the range of fabrics used. In eighteenth-century France – most especially in Paris and at Versailles – fashion was far from static: in fact, according to one chronicler of the period, it was in constant flux. Montesquieu observed that 'A woman who leaves Paris to spend six months in the country comes back as out of date as if she had been buried there for thirty years.'[1] During the reign of Louis XVI, these words found their visual counterpart in the work of a caricaturist who, when asked to sketch the characteristic dress of each of the nationalities of Europe, represented the Frenchman as naked, but carrying under his arm a parcel tied with string. On the parcel were written the words: 'Since this man's taste and clothes change from moment to moment, we have given him the fabric to use as he pleases, to dress himself as he wishes.'[2]

The satire was somewhat exaggerated, because often the changes that caught the imagination of Paris and the court were limited to such trivial matters as how one wore a scrap of lace or a flower. However, it is true that during the eighteenth century, fashion in France developed at a faster pace than ever before – a pace that accelerated as the Revolution approached.

Female Fashion

The summer of 1718 was a very hot one in France, hot enough, evidently, to encourage two stoutish French ladies to adopt the hooped petticoat that had already been in use in England for several years: they passed a hoop through the lower edge of their underskirts to keep the fabric away from their legs. During the same hot summer a fashion accessory appeared that was based on a garment worn by

1. *Distribution of Paniers in the Latest Style by Ma Mie Margot near Paris in 1735.* Musée de la Mode et du Costume, Palais Galliera, Paris. Margot was a dress-maker from Amboise. She invented a cheap way of making the fashionable huge, dome-shaped paniers in 1730 and can be seen here distributing them liberally.

French actresses of the period to give volume to their theatrical costume and to show off their waistline. This was the panier, so called because of its resemblance to a cage, 'a basket or panier (fig. 1) for poultry',[3] and composed of hoops made from plaited cord, small strips of metal or osier, or, more frequently, rings of whalebone attached together by ribbons.

About five years later the original panier was superseded by a petticoat made of gummed cotton or taffeta with about five hoops threaded through it (the English wore eight). The hoop at the top was called the *traquenard*[4] or 'trap' (in the vivid language of the day). Depending on its shape and size, which developed over the years and also changed at different times of day (to suit the wearer's occupation or mood), the panier was called a 'panier à guéridon' (a 'guéridon' is a small circular table), an 'elbow panier' (when it was very large and worn very high on the hips, presumably at a height to support the elbows), or a 'Jansenist' panier (named after the ascetic Catholic sect; when its modest size recommended it to women preferring a sober, more discreet style of dress). The small paniers worn in the morning, usually made from fabric stiffened with horse hair, were known as 'considerations'.

The panier was not new. It was closely related to the *vertugade* or farthingale, first worn in France in the early sixteenth century, at the time of François I, and it was to have a celebrated descendant in the crinoline of the Second Empire. In the eighteenth century it became the most important item in French fashion, the many stages of which were signalled by the various transformations of this garment; for although at this period masculine dress was still influenced by changing tastes and the development of the decorative arts, it was women who now set the tone.

The panier was not, however, solely responsible for moulding the female silhouette. The whaleboned bodice or stays arrived in France from Spain in the sixteenth century and consisted of a very rigid bodice reinforced in front by a long steel strip – denounced by Montaigne as an instrument of torture[5] – which narrowed the waist, raised the bust and forced the shoulders back. It moulded the upper

2. Maurice Leloir, *Histoire du costume de l'Antiquité à 1914.* Vol. XI: The reign of Louis XV, 1725–1774, Paris, 1938. Patterns for whaleboned bodices.

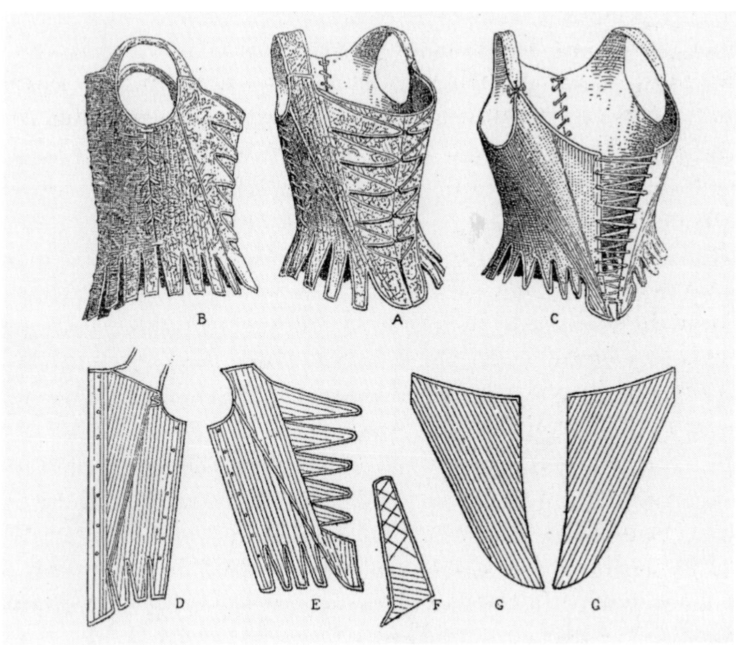

body so successfully that female children were forced to wear boned bodices as soon as they grew out of swaddling clothes, when their bodies were still malleable. Its presence explains the stiff posture of the women shown seated in paintings, unable to bend from the waist. When laced up the front, this boned bodice was called 'open', and when laced up the back, 'closed'. Pregnant women were permitted laces on the sides as well.

When, in 1795, boned bodices and paniers disappeared simultaneously, the Age of Enlightenment and such refinements of dress made their exit together. The fluid elegance of Greco-Roman antiquity was rediscovered, and for a time clothing followed the natural shape of the body.

From 1718 to1725

To begin with, the panier was quite discreet and small in size; it was simply a truncated cone measuring less than two ells (2m 40cm) in circumference at the hem and had the effect of flaring the dress slightly. It was worn only by rich women, as it could cost anything up to fifty pounds.

The *robe volante*, or flowing gown, featured by Watteau at the centre of his painting *L'Enseigne de Gersaint* of 1721, gave freedom and movement to the new fashion. In fact, it was not the style of the gown that was new, but the use to which it was put. Worn over the boned bodice and the petticoat, it had previously been worn only informally, in the privacy of the boudoir or bedroom, although its unwaisted shape sometimes made it the choice of pregnant women to disguise their condition (this, at any rate, was how it was worn by Madame de Montespan, whose little ruse fooled nobody: as soon as she appeared in the gown, the whole court realised immediately the nature of the happy event in prospect for the king's favourite mistress).[6]

The appearance of scores of such *robes negligées* in the streets shocked the older generation, who were accustomed to the stricter dress codes of Louis XIV. The Princess Palatine, in particular, found them 'impertinent' and would not allow anyone dressed in this way into her presence: 'It is as though the wearer is getting ready for bed', she declared in a letter of 12 April 1721.

Detail of fig. 3. Jean-Antoine Watteau, *L'Enseigne de Gersaint*. Schloss Charlottenburg, Berlin.

The gown fell slightly obliquely from the shoulders to the ground and was lifted in front by the hand, gracefully revealing the petticoat. The back was gathered or pleated across the shoulders to give fullness, the sleeves were pleated along their length, terminating below the elbow with a slightly flared cuff that revealed a sleeve of fine linen or lace. The gown perfectly expressed the spirit of the age, with its dreams of liberty and fluidity, joyfully repudiating the formality so dear to the Sun King.

Another, more traditional style of dress, which was associated with the reign of Louis XIV, was also in use. This consisted of a bodice opening to show the corset and a round skirt that might be a little longer behind than in front. The skirt was worn very tight at the waist and often had gathers held by straps below the waist at the back, or it could be bundled together artlessly in the hand at the back to shorten the train. Watteau depicted this style in his *Figures de mode*, his drawings from life and in *L'Enseigne de Gersaint* where it can be seen being worn by the older woman closely examining one of the paintings at the back of the shop. The customer seated in the foreground, beside the counter, is wearing the same type of dress. The style is reminiscent of the *manteau* or gown with a train attached to the waist which was worn at the time of Louis XIV; the shape was still to be found in the first quarter of the eighteenth century, echoed in the English *mantua*, with its two front panels that were drawn back and fastened behind (see below).

3. Jean-Antoine Watteau, *L'Enseigne de Gersaint*, 1721. Schloss Charlottenburg, Berlin.

From 1725 to 1740

From 1725 the panier began to increase considerably in size, ultimately adopting the shape of a huge dome which, by 1729, could measure as much as 3 ells (3m 60cm) around the base. Its size was beginning to cause trouble at court. One evening at the theatre, the queen, Marie Leczinska, who was very modest in her choice of paniers, quite literally disappeared behind the skirts of the princesses

who were accompanying her. Cardinal Fleury, the Prime Minister, ordered a seat to be left empty on either side of the queen and then, when the princesses complained, to leave a stool empty between them and the duchesses, who were, in turn, offended by the fact that no seat had been left vacant between them and the ladies of the next rank down.[7]

The Church, too, was disturbed by the fashion. One priest, Père Bridaine, devoted a whole sermon to the 'shamelessness and extravagance of the paniers worn by Christian women', threatening the 'unhappy women' who wore them with 'unprecedented misfortune and severe punishment from God in this world and the next'.[8]

Ignoring these threats, however, more and more women succumbed to the temptation of the panier. In 1729 the *Mercure de France* reported that even servants were going to market in paniers; this became more feasible after 1735 when a dressmaker in Amboise found a way of making them cheaply, thereby putting them within reach of all purses.

Over the domed panier, which gave them the appearance of a bell, women wore more or less the same clothes as before: a *robe volante* or flowing gown, 'open' or 'closed' (as depicted in the paintings of Jean-François de Troy); or alternatively a dress with a fitted waist. Less wealthy townspeople wore a full-backed jacket that matched the underskirt and was in fact no more than a *robe volante* cut off just below the hips.

Another type of bodice was also in use at this time. This consisted of a fitted jacket with a short basque and straight, elbow-length sleeves with large cuffs; it was completed by a stomacher worn over the chest and stomach. Such garments, made of plain fabric, can be seen in paintings by Watteau or Lancret,[9] where they are often worn by women dressed quite simply. The Musée de la Mode et du Costume de la Ville de Paris, in the Palais Galliera, contains two richly embroidered examples, dating from about 1730, and there is a third one, of later date to judge by the type of fabric used, which shows that the style survived until about 1755–60.

From 1740 to 1770

In about 1740 the panier became oval in shape – the result of a system of internal pulleys. At the same time, the *robe volante* changed radically, becoming fitted over the bust thanks to a coarse-cloth bodice lining that laced behind, below the pleats; the pleated back thus became a false cape reaching from the shoulders to the hem of the skirt and merging with the skirt at ankle level. The front of the gown was open at the top to show either the corset itself (if it was made of a fabric worthy of being seen) or a triangular stomacher that covered the corset. From the waist down the gown opened to reveal a matching underskirt or petticoat. The sleeves stopped short at the elbow

4 (above). Jean-François de Troy, *The Declaration of Love*, 1731. Schloss Charlottenburg, Berlin.

5 (left). Fitted *casaquin* with sleeve cuffs *en raquette*. Musée de la Mode et du Costume, Palais Galliera, Paris. This was worn with a stomacher and a long skirt, *c.*1740.

and terminated in a flared cuff, *en raquette*, that extended their length; below the cuffs a pair of so-called *engageantes* were worn. These were small sleeves with two or three flounces or lace frills, and longer over the elbows than on the bend of the arm; they had been worn since the end of the reign of Louis XIV. These developments culminated in the creation of the *robe à la française*, popular until the Revolution. Although the gown underwent a few modifications over the years, the characteristic pleats at the back persisted and have become known to modern historians as 'Watteau pleats', in honour of the memory of the most celebrated painter to depict them. In the eighteenth century they were simply called pleats.

In about 1750 the panier divided into two boned cages fastened together with cords or tape. These twin cages were very pronounced over the hips and became known as 'elbow paniers'[10] or 'comfort paniers' because the fore-arms could be rested on them.

Until about 1770 the *robe à la française* was the usual apparel of upper-class women, adapted to suit different circumstances by the quality of its fabric; it was worn by less well-off townswomen for special occasions; it was even to be seen on elegant maidservants, who wore it tucked into the pockets of the petticoat to make it less cumbersome. The cut remained the same, apart from a few details. The cuffed sleeves around the elbow were replaced by gathered flounces with scallops that complemented the serrated edges on the lace undersleeves most attractively. From 1765 onwards these flounces were sometimes replaced by a puff attached to the cuff, and the stomacher was also often replaced by two flaps of fabric that formed a false waistcoat fastened with buttons or hooks. The *robe à la française* was decorated around the front edges of the over-dress with puffs or with pleated bands stitched on in straight or wavy lines, or intertwined. The petticoat was frilled. The gown itself was liberally adorned with ribbons and lace and little bows of knotted silk. The slim-waisted, round-hipped silhouette produced by the gown and its fanciful decoration were the perfect expression of Louis-Quinze style.

In the middle of the century another style of dress was adopted by the fashionable élite. A French engraver, Hubert Gravelot, son of a Parisian tailor, returned to his homeland after spending twenty years in England and published a series of fashion plates that was largely responsible for the popularity of the new style. This was the *robe à l'anglaise* (known as the *mantua* in England, where it was very fashionable, particularly at court). The gown was made to be worn over circular hoops of modest size and was gathered at the back. As shown in Gravelot's drawings, and in surviving examples, the gown had a panel in the middle of the back that went from neck to hem in one piece; the panel consisted of pleats stitched flat at the top and waist and flowing freely in the skirt. The skirt was attached to the bodice on either side of the central panel by two semi-circular seams, one on each hip, and was pleated from the seams. At the front the skirt was detached to the bodice, which formed a point slightly below the waist, opening to reveal a separate stomacher. The skirt had no opening and was cut larger than the waistline; it was adjusted to the waist measurement by being gathered into a pleat on either side of the point of the bodice, and this gave the appearance of an overskirt opening to display an underskirt. One variation of the *mantua*, probably a little later in date, consisted of an underskirt and a skirt that opened on to it in front. This style of dress, in contrast to the *robe à la française*, showed a leaning towards simplicity and a desire (already beginning to emerge a few years earlier) to free the waistline. It marked one of the earliest manifestations of the mania for things English that was to grip France at the end of the century.

In paintings dating to around the middle of the century another type of female costume can be identified. This consisted of a full skirt, worn over hoops of varying size with a matching sleeveless boned bodice. The full sleeves of the chemise were revealed; these were tied with circles of ribbon halfway down and at the elbow, where they stopped. The outfit seems to be adapted from peasant costume, but

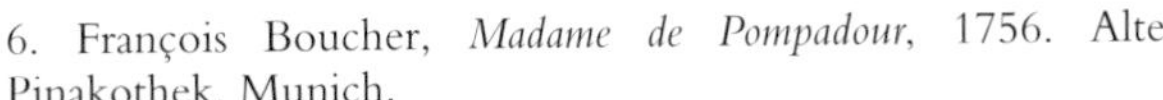

6. François Boucher, *Madame de Pompadour*, 1756. Alte Pinakothek, Munich.

the hoops (usually quite large) and the rich silk of which it was made give it an air of urban elegance. It can be seen in a portrait painted by Pierre Subleyras of his wife on the occasion of their marriage in about 1739.[11] There are different examples in other paintings by the same painter, but with sleeves made of the same fabric as the rest of the dress.[12] Boucher dressed Madame de Pompadour[13] and the woman assumed to be Madame Bergeret in the same style;[14] he gave both women the air of operatic shepherdesses, exaggerating this in the case of Madame Bergeret by showing her holding a large straw hat in her hand. Rather than a costume in daily use, in France at any rate, this seems to have been a costume for dressing up in: it lends an air of the nymphs and shepherdesses so popular in theatrical entertainment of the day.

From 1770 to 1781

As the century advanced, simplicity and ease of movement became more and more of a priority in city clothing. The *robe à la française* continued to be worn, but with a shorter petticoat and an overgown fastened at the neck rather than at the waist, under the influence of the *robe à la polonaise*, one of the styles that were beginning to compete with the French gown. The *robe à la polonaise*, which first appeared in 1775, consisted of a circular petticoat with a flounce round the hem, which reached to just above the ankle, and a dress cut like a waisted coat, fastened to the bodice in front and revealing the lower point of a small bodice below. At the back a system of cord pulleys allowed three panels of the dress (a tail and two wings) to be raised so that they fell in curves over the underskirt.[15] The sleeves were gathered in at the elbow and decorated with layers of lace. The success of this type of gown was due partly to the fact that it was worn over a bustle,[16] which was less constricting than a series of hoops and accentuated the hollow of the back. This new accessory was constructed of several layers of stout cotton stitched together; it derived from the gummed taffeta bustle worn under skirts at the end of the reign of Louis XIV and renowned for the creaking noise it made as its wearer moved.

An early version of the *polonaise* was depicted by Augustin de Saint-Aubin in 1773 in his painting *Le Bal paré*; two of the women seen dancing are wearing quite short dresses with overgowns fastened in

7. Engraving by G. Malbeste, after Moreau le Jeune, *La Sortie de l'Opéra* (detail), 1783. The woman on the left is wearing a *robe à la française*, the one on the right a *robe à la polonaise*. The back of the flower seller's dress is tucked into her pockets.

front by a false waistcoat and falling in curves over the petticoat, above the flounce at the hem. The type of dress shown is worn over a panier but fits the waist closely at the back. The cut of the gown is elegant and also very well suited to dancing because it has no train.

Variations on the *robe à la polonaise* included the *circassienne* and the *robe à la turque*. The Turkish style had a trailing skirt behind, whereas the Circassian was circular, but both comprised an overgown with very short sleeves beneath which the full-length sleeves of the underdress appeared. The *lévite* was a gown for informal wear with a large shawl collar and a long scarf worn round the waist and knotted loosely at the side.[17] These three styles bear witness to contemporary interest in the East (both Near and Far) and to a dream of distant lands that foreshadowed Romanticism.

Although the *robe à la française* was no longer as fashionable in town as it had been, it had its revenge over detractors of the *robe volante* by becoming (with a few modifications in the cut) the formal gown *par*

8a (above left). Engraving by Voysard, after Desrais, *Galerie des Modes et Costumes français* (reprinted by P. Cornu, plate 8). *Robe à la circassienne*, 1774.

8b (above right). Engraving by Dupin, after Leclerc, *Galerie des Modes et Costumes français* (reprinted by P. Cornu, plate 131). *Robe à la turque*, 1780.

8c (right). Engraving by Lebeau, after Leclerc, *Galerie des Modes et Costumes français* (reprinted by P. Cornu, plate 83). *Robe à la lévite*, 1779.

excellence. For ceremonial wear it was worn over large paniers. The bodice was very close-fitting and was fastened by lacing hidden under a fly front. The skirt followed the shape of the paniers at the sides and was attached to the bodice with the pleats and semi-circular seams already seen in the *robes à l'anglaise* depicted by Gravelot. The *robe à la française* was open in front over an underskirt and retained the pleats at the back (although these had become narrower); tradition was respected and the name 'French' was still well deserved.

The *robe à la piémontaise*, made fashionable at the time of the marriage of Princess Clotilde of France, sister of Louis XVI, to the Prince of Piedmont, was a variation on the *robe à la française*: the loose, flowing pleats at the back were added later to form a kind of cape attached behind.[18]

From 1782 to 1795

At the end of the eighteenth century the taste for simplicity and comfort was becoming more pronounced. In towns paniers disappeared completely, and with them the *robe à la française*. The whale-bone corset grew less tight. Doctors and hygienists, who had been waging war for years against the 'degradation of the human species' by this instrument of torture,[19] at last began to be listened to, thanks to the influence of Jean-Jacques Rousseau and the return to nature made fashionable by him. An unboned corset made of stout linen was occasionally worn as a substitute.

As a consequence of the passion for things English that gripped French society during this period, the *robe à l'anglaise* reappeared, slightly altered, with curved whalebone hoops at the waist; the overgown had a train and was open in front to show the underskirt and a small laced bodice. A large fichu adorned the shoulders, sometimes crossing over the chest and tying behind. The sleeves fitted the forearm tightly and small sleevelets of linen or lace were worn underneath.

From this outfit was derived a number of others that produced more or less the same silhouette: the *redingote* or riding-coat, tightly fitted and sporting revers on the bodice which were borrowed from masculine attire. The *demi-redingote* had the same revers, but the skirt was open in front. At this time the jacket or *caraco* (also known as the *juste à la Suzanne*), which was a *robe à l'anglaise* cut to hip-length, was worn with a skirt. The *pierrot* was another jacket with a small, full basque worn low at the back.

In the 1790s the circumference of gowns grew smaller. The waist was still in its natural place but was marked by a very broad belt that reached breast height. The breasts were hidden behind a curtain of fabric gathered on to a cord above and below. The long, tight sleeves reached half-way down the hands, like mittens.

Finally, one particular fabric was becoming increasingly fashionable. This was cotton muslin, white, light and transparent, which for

9 (right). François Watteau, called Watteau de Lille (attributed to), preparatory drawing for plate 281 of the *Galerie des Modes et Costumes français* (reprinted by P. Cornu, plate 198). Musée Carnavalet, Paris. Woman wearing a *robe à l'anglaise*, 1785.

10 (below left). Engraving by Dupin, after Desrais, *Galeries des Modes et Costume français* (reprinted by P. Cornu, plate 311). *Redingote à l'anglaise*, 1787.

11 (below right). *Journal de la Mode et du Goût*, 1792. Gown with a 'curtain' bodice.

years had been used to make simple, straight gowns with long, gathered sleeves and a wide ribbon round the waist. Marie-Antoinette and her friends wore dresses like this at the Trianon. Muslin was also used to make *caracos*[20] and skirts. As soon as muslin dresses were made without hoops and with the waist immediately below the bust – in 1795 – a new style was born, the 'Directoire', supposedly of classical inspiration.

Male Fashion

From 1719 to 1730

In the early years of the Regency the masculine three-piece outfit, which had been created at the end of the reign of Louis XIV, assumed the same sort of grace and charm that were characteristic of the period – a period dedicated to elegance and pleasure rather than to formality.

The outer garment, a collarless coat, was tight at the waist and flared over the hips. The skirt had four or five deep pleats on the hips and panels that widened almost to form a complete circle; it was knee-length and lined with cloth to keep its stiffness. It swung like a lady's dress when its wearer moved. Slits at the sides and mid-back allowed the hilt and the tip of the sword to pass through; the scabbard was worn under the coat on a strap. The sleeves were fairly short and ended in a broad winged cuff which was worn elegantly tight at the bend of the arm (fig. 4). Underneath was worn a long waistcoat with a thigh-length skirt and fitted sleeves extending to just beyond the sleeves of the coat. Although the front was often richly decorated, the back, invisible in wear, was made of plain fabric and in the centre was a laced slit whereby the waistcoat could be tightened for a close fit. The front had buttons and buttonholes from top to bottom, but only two or three of these – at waist level – were used because the jabot, or shirt frill, had to be prominently displayed at the neck. Like the coat, the waistcoat had two pockets just below the waist with decorated flaps that half covered the buttons (themselves purely decorative).

The breeches were mainly hidden by the outer garments. They were tight and were worn tucked inside the stockings which covered the knee. The back of the breeches was gathered into a small half-belt

12. Jacques-Louis David, *Antoine Lavoisier and his Wife*, *c.*1785. The Rockefeller University, New York.

positioned just below the waist. There were a number of chamois leather pockets and a plain front opening.

This three-piece outfit could be made in any fabric, from the most extravagant to the simplest, and was therefore adaptable to any social class. It became and remained for many years the mainstay of the male wardrobe. An ample mantle was added for going out; this cape, with its turned-down collar and no sleeves, had been made fashionable

Detail of fig. 3. Jean-Antoine Watteau, *L'Enseigne de Gersaint*. Schloss Charlottenburg, Berlin.

under Louis XIV by the duc de Roquelaure and was named after him. In 1725 the *redingote* (the French version of the English riding-coat) arrived from England: the *Mercure de France* described it in 1726 as 'a kind of large greatcoat, buttoned down the front, with a small cape and openings in front and at the sides . . . it is longer and fuller than the frock coat. When the king goes hunting in bad weather the lords accompanying him are all dressed in riding-coats. It is a garment well suited to horse riding and protects the wearer from the ill-effects of cold.'[21] It was a while before the *redingote* was adopted for town wear.

From 1730 to 1750

During the first half of the reign of Louis XV masculine dress lost some of the careless elegance it had adopted under the Regency; change came in nomenclature more than in shape. The jerkin now became known as the 'French suit' (*habit à la française*). This name was in use until the end of the Ancien Régime – or even later, since it was revived in the First Empire and the Restoration periods to designate court dress. It was to survive still longer as the name given to footmen's livery, which was cut to the same shape.

The coat was beginning to lose its fullness by this time: the side pleats measured only a quarter of a circle when laid flat and the waistcoat was growing shorter. From 1745 onwards the breeches were worn over the stockings and covered the knees. The garter closed with a small buckle that had its own buttonhole.

13. Jacques Dumont, known as Le Romain, *Madame Mercier, Wet Nurse to Louis XV, surrounded by her Family*, 1731. Musée du Louvre, Paris.

From 1750 to 1770

During the second half of the reign of Louis XV masculine dress became more linear (in the same way that the decorative arts had reacted against the Rococo). In the last portraits of Louis XV he is already dressed in what was to be called Louis-Seize style. In twenty years French clothing had shed a third of its fabric. The side pleats on the coat were gradually moving round to the back and the sleeves were becoming longer and narrower, with fewer ornamental facings; coat skirts became shorter.

At home a plain pair of breeches (black or coloured) would be worn with a dressing-gown and matching waistcoat, often made of fabric similar to that used for women's clothing. Sometimes just the waistcoat would be worn; this would be entirely made of silk or some similar, expensive fabric and would be designed to be seen on its own without a covering coat. Another favourite was the *apollon*, a short dressing-gown in light-coloured cloth, embroidered or brocaded in colour.

From 1770 to 1782

During the reign of Louis XVI the masculine silhouette became increasingly narrow. Coats developed a small stand-up collar, and the side pleats flattened and moved to the back. The sleeves of jackets grew tight and the cuff facings quite plain. Waistcoats, by now sporting only a short skirt or basque, began to be called *gilets* (fig. 21); the short basque revealed that the breeches now had a flap front and fitted waist. The three elements – coat, waistcoat and breeches – were still all worn together.

From 1782 to 1795

Clothes continued to grow tighter during the last decades of the century. Sleeves, for example, became so narrow that the wrists had to be slit to allow the hand to pass through. Armholes were cut further back into the torso, making the already very tight back even tighter. The coat front sloped off towards the back, as it does in a modern jacket, and the pleats (now completely flat) abutted the central slit in the back, lending no fullness to the silhouette of the coat. An increasingly high, straight collar imprisoned the neck. The waistcoat, with its short basque was, after 1783, almost invariably white and embroidered. It was fashionable to buy these by the dozen, with embroidery in a variety of styles. The breeches became ridiculously tight – quite 'immodest', according to Louis-Sébastien Mercier writing in 1788;[22] when he dressed in the morning, a dandy would have to jump upright into his breeches and would not be able to sit down or walk with large strides for fear of splitting the seams.

A clear distinction began to develop between court dress, still tradition-bound, and town dress, the latter yielding more readily than the former to influences from England and to the taste for novelty and fantasy; outfits were adopted in town that twenty years earlier would have been considered quite outré. One example of this was the *chenille*,[23] a silk velvet garment invented during the reign of Louis XV, apparently by the tailor Christopher Scheling (died 1761), and designed to be worn indoors. During the reign of Louis XVI dandies used to wear these over a pair of sailor's trousers as they made their way, incognito, about the town. This development, which began in 1778, had become fully accepted by 1787.

Other fashionable coats, worn with a long *gilet* with a squared-off bottom, a small stand-up collar and exaggeratedly large revers, often embroidered when other clothing was left plain, included the *frac*, with a collar that began straight but was later turned down; the *frac à*

14 (above left). Engraving by Dupin, after Desrais, *Galerie des Modes et Costumes français* (reprinted by P. Cornu, plate 138) (detail). *Redingote* with three collars and buttoned lapels.

15 (above right). Engraving by Duhamel after Defraine, *Magasin des Modes nouvelles françaises et anglaises* (detail), 1789. Informal dress.

l'anglaise, with tails at the back; the *habit-redingote*, very long and worn either over the *habit à la française* or directly over the waistcoat; and the *lévite* with buttoned revers (based on a military overcoat). In about 1790 the *lévite*, whose revers could be unbuttoned and fastened across the chest, evolved into a new item, the *dégagé* coat, which was very short in front and long behind. This style remained fashionable for many years; indeed, it is the prototype of modern evening dress.

During the French Revolution a short, straight garment arrived from Italy. This, known as the *carmagnole*,[24] was worn with a cross-over waistcoat and sailor's trousers. After 1792 it was one of the components of the garb of the *sans-culottes* (fig. 48).

Children's Fashion

Since children were dressed from a very early age in the same kind of clothes as their parents, for much of the eighteenth-century the layette was the only item specific to their wardrobe. The *maillot*[25] – a baby's entire wardrobe – included lots of swaddling clothes and napkins – squares or rectangles of cloth – in which the baby was tightly wrapped (often with only its head exposed) to protect it from cold and knocks and to prevent it from making any sudden movement that might (as was thought at the time) deform its fragile bones. Actual clothing was restricted to a few small vests, neckerchiefs, bonnets and bibs, the design of which is more or less timeless.

16. Antoine Raspal, *Madame Privat and her Two Daughters*, *c.*1778. Muséon Arlaten, Arles.

This babywear was used until the age of three, except for the bonnet which was replaced at six months by a small cap (*toquet*) for boys and a head-square for girls, which they continued to wear until they reached adolescence.

Between the ages of three and four, children of both sexes were dressed in a one-piece gown laced up the back, worn over a whalebone bodice (children, like adults, were squeezed into boned bodices). Boys' gowns had pleats stitched from shoulder to waist. Girls wore a gathered skirt attached to the lower bodice, the bodice forming a point in front. An apron, sometimes very elegant or, according to the social status of the child, simply worn for protection was added to the outfit; this had a bib that was pinned to the bodice.

At five years old a boy would receive his first pair of trousers, with a coat and waistcoat identical in every detail to those worn by men. The aristocracy liked to dress their children up in, for instance, Hungarian dress (fig. 29), heavy with frogging and derived from the clothes worn by pages or from military uniforms. In less wealthy families the coat was sometimes replaced by a shorter garment.

Girls kept their one-piece gowns, with leading reins fixed to the shoulders, for much longer. If the wearer belonged to the nobility or the upper bourgeoisie she would soon have to wear paniers and, on formal occasions, the *robe à la française*. The custom of early marriages, although not general, meant that some adolescent girls like Mademoiselle de FitzJames, who was married to the marquis de Maillé[26] at the age of thirteen, came out in society at the age of eleven, and therefore owned several ball gowns at a very young age. This may explain the tiny size of some of the dresses that have survived to this day: although having the appearance of women's clothing, their measurements indicate that they were made for children of about twelve years old.

It was only under Louis XVI that the influence of Jean-Jacques Rousseau began to be felt, reinforced by the naturalness and simplicity favoured by the English at the time. An interest began to be taken in children: concerns were voiced about their health and freedom of movement. As a result, their clothes became more functional. Boys wore sailor suits consisting of breeches, a straight waistcoat and a cutaway coat with a large ruched collar. Around 1787 girls, in imitation of English girls, wore straight dresses, often made of white muslin and tied with a broad sash around the waist.

Many museum collections of costumes contain miniature dresses,

17. Adolf Ulrik Wertmüller, *Marie-Antoinette and her Children in the Parc de Trianon*, 1785. National Museum, Stockholm.

often very richly decorated, with very short sleeves and wide necklines with a plunging slash in front; the side-seams are curved from the armholes as if to accommodate a panier. Some of these dresses were almost certainly made to clothe statues, since their sleeves are almost completely detachable to allow the arm to pass through. Others, with attached sleeves, may have been ceremonial baby's clothes at the time of Louis XV. However, I have never seen a child depicted dressed in this way.

Chapter 2

Underwear

Worn for reasons of modesty as well for hygiene, body linen or underwear also became at certain periods an important element of the overall appearance of clothing, particularly those parts of it that were visible. In the eighteenth century, underwear was relatively simple, its principle role being to support detachable lace accessories – fichus, shirt fronts and cuffs – which would simply be tacked on so that they could be removed easily and washed separately.

The essential item of underwear was the *chemise*,[1] which was always white, long and full. The chemises worn by the rich could be cut either in the French or in the English style. The French cut was fuller, the fullness being provided by four large gussets, two on each side stitched to the straight edges of the front panels to give a bias to the side seams from under the arms to the hem. The English-style chemise usually had gussets only to the waist, and gussets were sometimes placed head to tail, on one side only. This style suited only the slenderest women. Half sleeves, cylindrical in shape and gathered in at the elbow, were stitched to the shoulder with a straight seam. A small gusset under the arm allowed movement. The rectangular neckline with slightly rounded corners was wide enough to accommodate the head; nursing mothers would slash the neckline to the waist in the centre. A drawstring around the neckline allowed the chemise to be tightened to fit.

The chemise for men, or shirt, was equally geometric in cut. It also had a long opening in front to which the jabot was attached, and, besides the armhole gussets, a number of additional elements: a collar, two shoulder pieces (each with a gusset), and a heart-shaped patch at the base of the front opening. The jabot and cuffs would be stitched on only if they were made of muslin and could be washed at the same time as the chemise.

At night women would add a back-opening camisole or nightshirt, or a hip-length sleeping jacket with a pleated back, similar in shape to the French *casaquin*.

18. Engraving by Dupin, after Leclerc, *Galerie des Modes et Costumes français* (reprinted by P. Cornu, plate 49). Tailor fitting a fashionable boned bodice, 1778.

The wardrobes of the rich would contain an impressive number of chemises (a proper trousseau was supposed to include seventy-two). Petticoats, however, were much scarcer (the same trousseau containing only six underskirts); they were made of good-quality cotton or Indian dimity.[2] Owing to the fact that the same word was used for the petticoat and for what is today called a skirt, there is a certain amount of ambiguity in surviving inventories of clothing. A petticoat with matching *caraco* was sometimes worn in the house, made either of embroidered muslin or silk.

The eighteenth-century corset was (unexpectedly, considering the modern meaning of the word) not boned, and was also made of dimity.

Although it seems strange, given that this was a period when paniers held skirts away from the body, knickers or pantaloons were not worn by women. They were introduced into France by Catherine de Médicis, the wife of Henry IV, but were soon forgotten after her death. Women wore underpants for riding, generally black, under their long skirts, as evidenced by the posthumous inventory of Madame de Pompadour's wardrobe.[3] These were like men's trousers and had little in common with other items of body linen. On the other hand, Fragonard's painting *Le Verrou* shows men wearing white underpants under their trousers; these underpants were obtained from the hosier's when they were knitted and from the tailor's when they were made of cloth.[4]

Nightcaps and bonnets for wearing around the house, or during sickness or menstruation, were many and various: mob caps with a single row of lace, bigger bonnets with two rows of lace, head-bands and fillets were all important elements of a woman's wardrobe. Men wore tall nightcaps, gathered into a band at the front with a ribbon, like the one worn by Voltaire in the small painting showing him getting out of bed at his house at Ferney.[5]

CHAPTER THREE

Accessories

Accessories, very numerous and elegant in the eighteenth century, comprised all the items of clothing worn to embellish the main garments, to clothe parts of the body not covered by them, or to enhance the overall appearance of an outfit. For the sake of clarity, they are divided here into items worn on the body and items carried in the hand. They reflect the development of taste and, on occasion, of customs.

ACCESSORIES WORN ON THE BODY

Complements to the Main Garments

The ruffles worn by women and known as *engageantes* have already been discussed. These ruffles, consisting of two or three layers of lace, first appeared in about 1705 and were worn under the scalloped sleeves of the *robe à la française* almost until the end of the century. The ruffles were partnered by a neck-piece (either a ruff or a cravat, often with matching lace) stitched around the neckline of the chemise; the neck-piece would be made of lace – from Alençon, Argenton or Valenciennes, or from England.

When simpler gowns came into fashion under Louis XVI, cuffs, ruffles and neck-pieces were often made of gauze and would be attached directly to the dress. The nicknames given in French to different kinds of cuffs and ruffles (*maris*,[1] *mirfats, petits bonshommes*) give little clue to the exact shape of the objects they designate. At this period fichus (triangles or diagonally folded squares in white muslin or gauze) began to be worn to cover the neckline; these were a version of the fichus already worn by women of the lower classes. In about 1745 a short cape came into fashion; it had two extended front panels which crossed over the chest and were tied at the back. As the French Revolution approached, the fichu increased in size, giving the bust the appearance of being ampler than it really was.

19.
Anonymous,
Françoise-Marie Pouget, Second Wife of Jean-Baptiste Chardin.
Musée Carnavalet, Paris.

During the so-called Romantic era a small starched ruff first appeared. This was called a *médicis* in memory of the high collar worn by Catherine de Médicis. The earliest visual references to Antiquity began to be made about this time also, when the waistline rose to just under the bust and was bound with ribbon.

During the Regency the palatine came into fashion. This was a small fur cape, a copy of the one favoured by the Princess Palatine, sister-in-law of Louis XIV. This was followed by the *mantelet*, a short cape of varying length, made of cotton or silk and sometimes having a *coqueluchon* or hood attached.

One indispensable accessory for men, besides the ruffles and jabot fastened to the shirt, was the cravat, which made its appearance in 1678 and owed its name to a regiment of Croats maintained by Louis XIV: the soldiers revived the Roman habit of wearing a scarf knotted round their necks. In the eighteenth century this consisted of a long strip of white linen that encircled the neck and fastened behind. Until about 1730 the two black ribbons of the wig were brought over the cravat and tied under the chin (fig. 20).

During the Revolution the cravat became a scarf worn tied round the high, pointed collar of the shirt and knotted at the throat.

As discussed above, children were dressed as adults from a very early age; the only accessory specific to their age group was the bib of the layette, like a broad stomacher, and the lace collar worn by small boys on their sailor suits at the end of the reign of Louis XVI.

Hats, Bonnets, Hair-styles

The shape of headgear is nearly always dictated by the hair-style of the wearer. During the Regency and under Louis XV men continued to wear wigs. The wig worn at the time of Louis XIV was still being worn in 1730 by old people, as well as by members of some professions, of which they became the symbol. The Louis XV wig was always powdered, which had its drawbacks on very windy days;[2] it was worn just behind the hair-line and the hair was brushed back over it to conceal the join on the forehead. Layers of rolled curls on either

20. Engraving by C.-N. Cochin, after J.-F. de Troy, *Le Jeu de pied de boeuf* (detail), 1725. Notice the man's bag wig with black ribbons that tie round the cravat; he wears high shoes with small buckles. The women are wearing small lace caps and high-heeled shoes.

21. Engraving by Duhamel, after Watteau fils, *Galerie des Modes et Costumes français* (reprinted by P. Cornu, plate 233). Young man-about-town in a *lévite anglaise*, wearing a round hat and English boots, 1786.

side, called *ailes de pigeon* ('pigeons' wings'), hid the ears. The way the hair was arranged at the back determined the style of the wig. When the back hair was enclosed in a small black taffeta bag (fig. 20) the wig was a 'bag wig'. The back hair was also sometimes divided into three small pigtails, the middle one being rolled and the outer two plaited; the *queue* consisted of two plaited or ringletted pigtails tied together with a ribbon. By about 1755 the horizontal curls at the side had been reduced to two layers and the ears could just be seen. The *catogan* was a single pigtail tied with a black bow. In about 1785 the layers of horizontal curls were replaced by curls going right round the head. During the Revolution powdered wigs, and in fact wigs in general, went out of fashion; Robespierre, who continued to wear a wig, was the exception, remaining loyal to a habit that in fact was by now considered aristocratic.

The wearing of wigs did not make the wearing of hats very easy and for a time hats were carried under the arm more frequently than they were worn on the head. (In 1761 a certain Monsieur Prevost, a hatter, of Rue Guénégaud in Paris, was making 'hats of silk and demi-silk, in all shapes, to wear under the arm or on the head'.[3]) For most of the eighteenth century felt hats were worn exclusively by men, women borrowing the men's fashion only when they went riding. The most popular style was the three-cornered hat, which first appeared in 1710, growing smaller in size under Louis XV (at which time it was renamed the *lampion* or 'lantern'). Derived from this, under Louis XVI, were the Swiss hat (with two long points on either side and a vestigial one in the middle of the front) and the 'Androsman' hat, higher and more compact. Also worn during this period were the Walachian hat or *chapeau en clabaud*, whose brim turned up at the back, and the Pennsylvanian hat, with a broad, slightly upturned brim. 'Dutch' or 'quaker' hats and 'jockey' or 'Jacquet' hats were round; the Dutch hat had a broad brim, the 'jockey' a narrower one, but both were ancestors of the top hat, with its cylindrical crown, which appeared just before the Revolution.

Apart from the tricorn and the shepherdesses' straw hat as worn by Madame de Pompadour for walking in the garden, the traditional headgear for women was the cap; for going out this was covered by the *coqueluchon*, or by a *mantelet* or mantle, all short capes worn instead of a coat. The covering of the head was a survival from an oriental custom, brought to the west by the Church: married women were forbidden to show their hair because it was considered seductive.

Caps were worn for reasons of coquetry and followed the modifications of the hair-style. When tiny curls all over the head were in

22. Anonymous engraving, *Journal de la mode et du goût*, 15 December 1790. Woman carrying a muff shaped like small barrel, wearing a sugar-loaf hat.

fashion during the Regency and at the beginning of the reign of Louis XV, fashion-conscious women wore only a scrap of lace on their heads. By the middle of the century, when hair was worn high and padded, and a series of small, horizontal ringlets one on top of the other framed the face, caps were worn only in the house; they were subsequently demoted, becoming the headwear of the urban middle classes and of servants. This was the era of the *baigneuse*, the *dormeuse*, the *cornette*, the *battant l'oeil*, and the *bonnet à bec* – also called the *cabochon*, as worn with a mantle over it by Queen Marie Leczinska when reading in her rooms – which made an elegant peak on the forehead (fig. 43). These caps, with their circular crowns gathered into a headband with ruffled edges, often had two long lace streamers which would be pinned up on the top of the head for comfort, thus concealing what was often magnificent, hand-made lace.

After the accession of Marie-Antoinette, headdresses, already tending to grow taller, were driven as if by some irresistible force to greater and greater heights. Hair, hair-pieces, various ornaments and a cap surmounting the coiffure were all stacked up so that the woman's chin was 'half way to her feet', as the Baroness d'Oberkirch jokingly remarked. Soon two hundred distinct types of headgear could be counted amongst the stock of fashionable milliners like Rose Bertin or Beaulard. 'Every week new structures can be seen on women's heads. We particularly liked the caps in the Parc Anglais: we saw windmills, woodland groves and streams, sheep, shepherds and shepherdesses, a hunter in a copse', wrote Sébastien Mercier in about 1782. To cover these structures, the *coqueluchon* expanded to become the *thérèse* or the *calèche*, supported by hoops like the roof of a carriage.

Women finally grew tired of having to ride in carriages on their knees or of holding their heads outside the door because their headgear could not be accommodated inside, and they lowered the height of their headgear. A more pressing reason for doing so, perhaps, was the fact that the queen had lost all her hair in giving birth to the Princess Royal and had started the fashion for a new broad, low hairstyle like that worn by children. The high cap was now often replaced by a fichu of draped gauze, trimmed with two or three upright ostrich feathers.

The most significant item introduced during the period was the milliner's hat. It would enjoy a dazzling career and eventually outshine men's hats, which were becoming more and more sober in style. In 1778 a band began appearing at the base of certain caps; it

23. Engraving by Dupin, after Leclerc, *Galerie des Modes et Costumes français* (reprinted by P. Cornu, plate 146). Young girl wearing a shift of painted linen, tucked up *à la polonaise*. The boy in the centre is wearing a sailor suit; the baby is wearing an English cap or *toquet*, 1780.

either covered a circle of brass wire or was made of woven straw. The crowns of the caps were still soft, but the rigid brims now made them officially into hats. In about 1785 real hats began to be worn on top of big, bouffant hair-styles that offered the ideal support for them. These hats were made of straw or fabric, stretched over card or brass (figs 8 and 10); they had broad brims and high, cylindrical crowns and bore some relation to the big 'musketeers' hats of the reign of Louis XIII, if only by virtue of their size. These hats came into fashion at a time when women were wearing coats of slightly masculine cut. In 1790 fashions changed, however, and the sugar-loaf crown became popular – a preliminary adaptation of the style that was to be followed by dozens of others.

Children had no particular headgear except for the *bourrelet* or 'pudding', a small fitted cap with a padded sausage around the crown to protect the child's head from knocks. Between six months and four years of age, small boys wore a little cap called a *tocquet*.

Gloves and Muffs

Gloves were not worn universally in the eighteenth century. Contemporary manners decreed that they should be removed at certain times: when one was meeting a social superior; when eating; when entering a church; when extending ones hand to give or receive anything. Forgetful hunters who did not remove their gloves when they returned to the stables would be fined by the ostlers. Hunt whippers-in would impose the same fines at the kill.

Nevertheless, gloves made of leather, silk or yarn were worn to complete an outfit; for indoor wear, fingerless lace mittens were worn. In winter gloves were lined with fur (marten or ermine); in spring, with curled feathers. In summer white gloves woven in lisle from Cologne were preferred. Silk disappeared from view for a short time in 1790 because of a doctor's claim that it dried the skin. In the early days of the Revolution chamois leather gloves had slogans printed on them – 'Vive le Roi', 'Vive la Nation, l'Union, la Liberté, 1789' – with a vignette representing Liberty sitting in front of the altar of Peace.

The muff, 'for putting hands in to keep them warm' in Furetière's definition, made its first appearance in France in the second half of the sixteenth century. It was still very fashionable in the eighteenth, whether made of fabric (the so-called Jesuit muff) or, more frequently, of fur. Initially, muffs were long and straight, but during the reign of Louis XV they expanded in size and adopted a variety of different shapes. Just before the Revolution they reached absurd proportions, for women as well as for men, who wore them round their necks on a string. Owing to their shape they were nicknamed 'little barrels' (fig. 22). Women's muffs later reduced in size and were decorated with frills and flounces; inside the muff a box of powder could be secreted, a handkerchief or a tobacco pouch or occasionally even a small animal, a lap dog or a small monkey. Muffs were worn in the street and to the opera and balls.

Stockings and Shoes

The masculine fashion for wearing breeches and, under Louis XVI, the feminine fashion for shorter skirts gave the stocking its moment of glory. Stockings derived from medieval hose, of which they represented the lower half, covering the legs and feet only. From 1656 onwards they were made on a loom. In the eighteenth century white stockings were the fashion, either in silk with gold embroidery or in yarn embroidered with wool; striped and chiné stockings were also available. During the Revolution clocks were multicoloured and very broad, often representing stylised foliage. Men wore black stockings even when not in mourning.

Women wore garters – consisting of a ribbon tied just above the knee – to hold up their stockings. Under Louis XVI garters became more elaborate and could take the form of a small satin bracelet in two halves, one bearing small springs inside to act as elastic, the other decorated with embroidery and, frequently, amorous devices,[4] similar in design to men's coat buttons.

At the beginning of the century the heels of men's shoes were very high but suddenly became lower in 1726. The heels of the aristocracy remained red, however, adhering to the regulation established under Louis XIV. Square toes became round (fig. 20). Large silver buckles on shoes were the height of fashion, but it was stated in the *Mercure de France* that 'truly elegant men wear diamond buckles'.[5] During the reign of Louis XVI the shape of the shoe did not alter, but heels continued to get lower and buckles grew in size, becoming so large that they almost filled the whole upper (fig. 12) and often caused injury to the ankles, according to the comte de Vaublanc.[6] Having put up with the painful consequences of fashionable footwear with great fortitude, the comte was eventually obliged to give it up and thereafter to suffer sarcastic comments about the small size of his buckle – which required even more courage.

Top boots arrived in France from England in about 1779, but were not widely adopted until the beginning of the Revolution (fig. 21).

During the Regency, women's shoes were pointed and had very high heels (fig. 20). They were made of embroidered leather, or of fabric to match the other garments. They were decorated with small, square buckles threaded through two straps. Heels decreased in height under Louis XV, but the shoe or mule (fig. 18), retained its elegant curved lines. During the reign of Louis XVI the heel, by then quite low, moved forward towards the instep; with nothing very durable to strengthen the sole, elegant shoes had a tendency to collapse under the weight of their wearer. By the 1780s women were making positive jewel caskets of their shoes, with emeralds and other precious stones all over the tongues – now called in French *venez-y-voir*, 'come and have a look'. During the Revolution shoes grew more and more pointed and heels almost disappeared.

⋆ ⋆ ⋆

Accessories Carried in the Hand

Bags and Purses

Handbags were almost unheard of in the eighteenth century because the fullness of the hooped skirts made it possible to wear capacious pockets; these were reached through slits in the sides of the gown and were attached to the underskirt. They contained all the small objects that a woman might need during the course of the day. At most, especially during the reign of Louis XVI, a small fabric work-bag might be carried, or a small card-holder embroidered with amorous mottos or courtly conundrums.

In the early part of the century money-purses were simply small bags finely embroidered with pearls – a speciality of France that was in demand abroad. They later became more oblong in shape and were made of printed or embroidered fabric, or silk lattice decorated with ribbons and braid.

Handkerchiefs

Although the handkerchief is basically a utilitarian object, its use did not spread to all classes of society until the seventeenth century; it could also be a fashion accessory. Ménage, in his *Dictionnaire étymologique*, advised women to call theirs a 'pocket handkerchief' rather than a handkerchief for blowing the nose.

One of the daughters of Louis XV had two dozen handkerchiefs trimmed with 'English and Alençon lace', certainly designed to be worn ceremonially. Handkerchiefs performed an important function at dances, when young ladies had to learn how to pass them gracefully from one hand to the other during different dance steps.

Men had a choice between white handkerchiefs and big snuff-takers' handkerchiefs in dark colours, sold first by the Compagnie des Indes, and then, from 1760, printed in France.

Fans, Umbrellas and Parasols

The fan is thought to have been invented in China between 2,700 and 2,250 BC. The first fans arrived in France in the fourteenth century, but their use did not become widespread until the seventeenth century; the eighteenth century was one of the most glorious periods for the fan.

During the reign of Louis XV the fan was usually made of vellum[7] painted in pale colours; the frame was generally made of ivory or mother-of-pearl, elaborately carved. Later in the century frames grew plainer and more delicate. The vellum was now often replaced by taffeta decorated with painted medallions alternating with embroidered panels; the subjects were romantic or (particularly during the Revolution) topical.

Like the handkerchief, the fan was carried in the hand; it was used to complement the ensemble, but fans also gave rise to a whole sign language which was taught in a special academy in London. At court it was forbidden to open a fan in the presence of the sovereign unless one was making a presentation, in which case it was used as a tray.[8] At the theatre the fan allowed people to watch others without being seen – that is, after the invention in 1759 of lorgnette fans with a small lens in the hinge, and peeping fans with transparent windows in them through which everything could be surreptitiously observed.

At the time of Louis XIV, parasols and umbrellas were heavy and awkward. They were used for protection from both sun and rain but were not in general use. In 1710, however, Jean Marius invented a collapsible umbrella that could be folded and put in a sheath like the modern umbrella, and could be carried in the pocket.[9] Forty or so years later a Monsieur Navarra invented a walking-stick umbrella – a walking stick which contained an umbrella.

It is not known if these gadgets were in widespread use, but it seems doubtful, given the description in 1768 by the oratorian Caraccioli of a Parisian carrying an umbrella uncomfortably 'under his arm for six months, during which time he might use it six times'. 'Those who dislike being mistaken for the common herd', he adds, 'prefer running the risk of getting wet to being spotted in the street looking like persons who travel everywhere on foot: the umbrella is a tell-tale sign of someone who has no carriage.'[10] It was probably for this reason that, in 1769, someone came up with the idea of providing public umbrellas on loan when crossing the bridges of Paris – more exposed to bad weather or sunshine than the streets, which were at that time very narrow.[11] At the end of the century the umbrella became a patriotic symbol: they were white in 1788, green in 1789, and red in 1791. In 1796 a loop was fixed to the handle so that the umbrella could be hung on the arm.

Throughout the century the parasol was small and edged with fringes or lace. Madame de Pompadour owned one adorned with Chinese scenes on mica and paper. Mademoiselle Bertin is said to have worn one perched on top of her coiffure. The simple small parasol with a plain straight handle could be used as a stick when closed and held pointing down; even the simplest of these would be brightened up with charming decorations.

Canes

At the beginning of the eighteenth century, canes were often made of rattan imported from the east. In his *Dictionnaire du Commerce* (1773), Savary states that they were 'decorated at the top with gold or silver, agate or ivory handles, or (more frequently) with knobs of different kinds of wood. There is another kind of knob called a 'lorgnette' which has two lenses, one at either end, an ocular lens and an objective lens; these serve as a kind of spy hole, allowing the stick-bearer to see objects that are at a distance'.

Voltaire and Dr Tronchin carried very long canes with gold knobs; these were in demand amongst old people, magistrates and financiers. Young people adopted the switch, a shorter, pliable cane, as they went about town in their morning 'undress'. Women also used canes, particularly when following their doctor's orders and going for a morning walk; their canes were made of bamboo, elegantly decorated with gold, and were held in the middle.

In the 1790s the well-dressed man carried a stout cane lashed with cat-gut and concealing a blade. A little later Jacobins were in the habit of carrying a sort of knotty cudgel.

Chapter Four

Fabrics and their Decoration

It is self-evident that without fabric there would be no costume; at any rate, without fabric costume would have been quite different in appearance. By the eighteenth century the animal skins worn by our ancestors had become elegant furs which, although sometimes used to add warmth to winter garments, were worn principally for their appearance. In the eighteenth century fur clothing was sometimes contrived to imitate silk. The armour worn by medieval knights now survived only in the shape of a cuirass or breastplate, worn during battle by the king and his officers. This garb was more ceremonial than practical, since it would not really have withstood cannon fire. Portrait painters loved the breastplate, however, for the way it added martial bearing to their noble models.

Fabrics generally give some idea of the use to which a garment is going to be put, whether body linen or outer garments, working clothes or festive wear, clothing for minor entertainments or for ceremonial occasions. Fabrics are also markers of social class, indicating if their wearers are noble, middle or working class, although by the eighteenth century the sumptuary laws that restricted expenditure on 'luxuries' such as clothes were in abeyance, and clothes expressed mainly the state of their wearer's purse.

Linen and Cotton

Underwear was made from the type of linen known as 'holland', originally made in the Netherlands but by the eighteenth century woven all over France, and from cotton: fustian, dimity, Indian muslin.[1] Cotton had not yet achieved quite the importance it was to achieve later, but it had been in use in western Europe since the sixteenth century; during the seventeenth century 'mechanical methods of spinning and weaving were in place'.[2] Parisian washerwomen were apparently famed for being able to reduce these light fabrics to shreds in a few weeks, with their heavy-handed use of the scrubbing brush and battledore; as a result, few examples survive today. Only a few, very elegant pieces that would have been worn externally still exist, including caps, cravats and ruffles whose embroidery and lace obviously inspired greater respect in the laundresses.

White Embroidery

Embroidery signifies the addition of decoration, by means of needlework, to a fabric. The decoration may be of gold or silver thread, silk or wool for outer garments, but was generally white cotton for underwear. During the reign of Louis XV *engageantes*, cravats and caps were embroidered with foliage executed in running stitch or with grids worked on pale muslins, whose 'threads were drawn together in different combinations and stitched in regular patterns'. Sometimes two muslins would be stitched together following a paper pattern placed under the fabric';[3] a relief effect was achieved by cutting away one of the two layers of muslin. At the end of the century simple chain-stitch flowers were embroidered in the squares on cotton net.

Lace

Lace is made either with a hook and thread, or with a row of threads spooled on bobbins, the threads being interwoven to form a net; as the eighteenth century advanced the net grew progressively finer. Lace was invented in the sixteenth century simultaneously in Italy and Flanders and, thanks to the combined efforts of Louis XIV and his controller-general of finance, Jean-Baptiste Colbert, it became a luxury product in seventeenth-century France. By the reign of Louis XV it had achieved an elegant balance between the splendid architectural style of the reign of Louis XIV, more suitable for large objects than for small toilet accessories, and the slightly over-pretty frivolity of certain types of lace made during the reign of Louis XVI. Alençon and Brussels produced needle laces; Valenciennes, Binche and Brussels (again), bobbin laces: these towns gave their names to costly creations covered in intertwined garlands of flowers, of varying degrees of extravagance.

Unfortunately much of this lace has now been unpicked. To gain some idea of what the lace accompaniments that were the indispensable complement to any elegant costume (masculine or feminine) looked like, contemporary portraits should be studied. Portrait painters of the day were eager to reproduce these small masterpieces of handicraft in minute detail. There was, moreover, lace for all seasons: thicker needle lace for winter, lighter bobbin lace for summer.

Wool and Knitwear

In the eighteenth century the French cloth-manufacturing industry fell into recession following the departure of a significant proportion of its predominantly protestant workforce after the revocation of the Edict of Nantes in 1685. The recession was accentuated by the fact that the court was wearing more and more silk. Nevertheless, the custom of wearing mourning, and the Anglomania that, during the reign of Louis XVI, imposed woollen clothing on everyone, including courtesans, kept the industry ticking over. Woollen fabrics like serge, ratine, flannel and flannelette were much used, as were those with less familiar names: *calemande*,[4] used for petticoats and dressing-gowns, drugget, *dauphine*[5] for summer clothes; for the winter there were *pinchina* from Spain, rash, Sommières from the town of the same name and *revêche*,[6] used for lining the uniforms of the King's army and for making winter petticoats.

The damage caused by moths means that little trace of these woollen garments remains. Those that have survived are often made of rather coarse, rough cloth; exceptions are the clothes designated as 'semi-formal', which consisted of wool combined with gold and silver embroidery.

Knitted fabrics were used for bonnets and caps, stockings, gloves and underwear, and also for the trousers worn under the skirt when women went riding. A number of masculine garments were made of knitted silk, either black or coloured.

Silk

Silk enjoyed a tremendous vogue: taffetas, twills, satins and plain velvets, and of course the extravagantly brocaded silks. The silk industries of Lyon – at that time the principle provider of silk fabrics worn at court – Tours – the oldest silk-weaving centre but now rather overshadowed by Lyon – and Paris – which also had its own workshops – were celebrated throughout the world. Proof of the fame of French silk is provided by the collections of fabric samples from French factories, gathered together on the orders of Maréchal Richelieu in 1735 and 1736 and preserved in the Print Room of the Bibliothèque Nationale de France. Two satins to be found there, one with 'light yellow background, sprigged with a thousand flowers', and the other 'striped', were worn by the queen, Marie Leczinska. Another fabric in the collection, 'costing 144 *livres* the ell', is gold and bears 'big flowers with bright gold centres and petals in purple, mauve, lilac and brown chenille with touches of matt gold'. This was purchased in Paris, with some others costing only 30 *livres* the ell, by King John v of Portugal.

Today, even when documentary information can be found, it is not easy to trace with any certainty the origin of the silks from which surviving garments are made. The problem of dating the fabric is complicated further by the custom of re-using fabrics. Brocaded silks were expensive. They were considered important possessions and were mentioned in marriage contracts and posthumous inventories of property. Even when they were out of fashion, clothes were stored very carefully. If a gown was still worth wearing it could be altered and brought up to date; in such cases there is sometimes a time-lag of ten or even fifteen years between the date of the manufacture of the fabric and the style and cut of the gown. Nevertheless, a large number of clothes, many of them of the most opulent kind, show no sign of having been re-used. This probably indicates that they came from the wealthiest households, where wardrobes would be renewed frequently and comprehensively. The costume collection in the Palais Galliera (the library of the Musée des Arts décoratifs) in Paris provides abundant information about the silk manufacture of the period and its products.

Men's clothing at the time of Louis xv could be made of brocaded cloth, cut velvet[7] backed by brocade, or plain velvet, in colours ranging from brown to almond green and including some very vivid reds. The clothes were often embellished with embroidery in gold and silver or in silk. From 1750 coloured paste jewellery was also used.

Sometimes the outline of an outfit would be woven into the fabric: the pattern of the garment appeared on the piece of fabric and only one outfit could be made from that piece. The tailor would cut

24. Waistcoats woven to shape, *c.*1750–55. Musée de la Mode et du Costume, Palais Galliera, Paris.

out the coat and waistcoat and adjust them to his client's figure; after that the pocket-facings and cuffs, woven separately, would be stitched on and the breeches cut from what remained of the material.

A taste for lighter-coloured silks, in beige or mauve, developed under Louis XVI. Pale blues and pinks, buttercup yellows and *caca dauphin* came into fashion and, as the Revolution approached, fine multi-coloured stripes. Quite a lot of taffetas, watered silks and corded velvets were made in plain colours. Others, known as *miniature* velvets, had small patterns woven into them, and these were often picked out with 'needlework painting' – coloured silk embroidery in *passé* (padded stitch) or chain stitch.[8] The designs varied in size and aimed at creating very naturalistic effects.

From 1783 a new fashion in waistcoats emerged: now an embroidered white waistcoat was *de rigueur*, in satin or in faille (known as *gros de Naples*) according to the season. These were often worn with a plain coat and breeches. The striking number of waistcoats of this type to be found in museums bears witness to the craze for embroidered flowers or scenes. In her *Mémoires*, Madame d'Oberkirch com-

25a (above left). Damask. Private collection, Paris.

25b (above right). *Cannetillé*. Private collection, Paris.

25c (right). Brocade. Private collection, Paris.

ments: 'They are exceptionally expensive but everybody wants them.' Most of the embroidery was done in silk factories, where there was a staff of watercolourists and embroiderers: watercolour sketches of designs for waistcoats, very evidently the handiwork of a single team, can be found today in the Palais Galliera in Paris, and in the Metropolitan Museum of Art and the Cooper Hewitt Museum[9] in New York. Clients would choose from pattern books. Pre-embroidered waistcoats were often sold unfinished, ready to be handed over to the tailor – just like the pre-woven pieces that had been sold earlier in the century. The same process was applied to men's clothes and women's gowns, which explains why identical items of clothing can be found in geographically distant places.

During the eighteenth century it was women's wardrobes that used the most varied and sumptuous silks, although the looms of this period did not perform particularly well and the presence of several assistants around the weaver was required. Men used the same silks only for their dressing-gowns. These silks can be divided into several large groups, according to their decoration; the groups mingled and merged as time went by.

First, the fabrics with large designs, derived from late seventeenth-century furnishing fabrics, with lace patterns embellished with palmettes, flowers and large fruit (of these, the pomegranate was the favourite) placed symmetrically on either side of a central line. The best examples of these date from the 1720s. The pattern joins were sometimes almost sixty centimetres apart – proof that little distinction was made at the time between 'furnishing' and 'dress' fabrics.

At the same time damasks in matching tones were popular; these bore large flower designs, generally very natural-looking roses or peonies. Two *robes volantes*, one in the Palais Galliera, the other in the Costume Institute of the Metropolitan Museum of Art, are made from fabrics of this type.[10]

In the 1730s the silks nicknamed '*bizarres*', which had been in fashion since 1715 and had 'Italian style' written all over them (they strongly reflected the Italian taste for baroque ornamentation and extravagant patterns), began to inspire the French to design small landscapes on fabrics, against a background foil of large plants or objects. Fabric of this type, and it is impossible to be quite sure if the one in question is Italian or French, can be seen on a gown in the Musée de la Mode et du Costume in Paris; the silk is decorated with large designs of flowers, fruit, viols, musical scores in which the stave and the notes can be clearly made out, painters' palettes and brushes and small landscapes with trees and arches. Both the gown and the fabric date from about 1740.[11]

Around 1750 other foreign influences became apparent. The influence of China, also to be seen in other branches of the decorative arts at the time, can be discerned on one *robe à la française* decorated with sprays of strawberries and small triangular motifs, the latter apparently taken from some Far Eastern book of designs. This was also the period when pagodas, pavilions and bridges were dotted liberally over women's shoulders, as they would soon be dotted all over the ornamental gardens of the aristocracy. A very original *robe à la française* in the Palais Galliera collection[12] shows this oriental influence: it is of yellow silk-satin, with rows of slightly stylised carnations, typically Turkish, alternating with rows of a kind of Kashmir palm-leaf design, the top of the palm-leaf being tousled like a sunflower.

The taste for sprays of flowers evolved in about 1735; it can be seen on a magnificent outfit in the Palais Galliera of (to judge by its shape and the facing on the sleeves) approximately the same date.[13] By 1745 the sprays had developed into sinuous garlands of naturalistic flowers,[14] soon to be mixed with the ribbon, fur and lace patterns that persisted until 1765. This frequently recurring theme is abundantly represented in museums: its use on dress fabrics coincided with the full flowering of the decorative arts during the reign of Louis XV.

Striped fabrics began to make their appearance in the 1760s.[15] Their use increased in the mid-1770s, when the stripes were often combined with small sprigs of flowers. By about 1780, however, such ornamentation had virtually gone out of fashion.

Throughout the century well-dressed men and women had at their disposal fabrics that were masterpieces. However, the designers and silk weavers who were responsible for them have for the most part remained anonymous. Some designers from the silk factory in Lyon[16] are better known, either because they were also writers, like Joubert de l'Hiberderie, Dutilleu, Dechazelle or Paulet (who came from Nîmes), or because they were so much admired by their contemporaries. In the latter category are included Pierre Ringuet, the first person to draw flowers from nature (in about 1730); Courtois, the first designer to use polychrome; Revel, remarkable for having invented a new technique of brocading that produced results closely resembling embroidery; Philippe de Lasalle, renowned especially for his furnishing silks; and Jean Pillement who specialised in chinoiserie.

It is also known that these designers used to go to Paris, where fashion was formed, twice a year to visit the shops of the tailors, milliners and dressmakers in the Rue Saint-Honoré. They also wanted to see theatrical costumes, to look at flowers painted by artists and flowers grown in the Jardin des plantes, to study botany, to buy prints and drawings and to visit the Gobelins tapestry factory, the Savonnerie carpet factory and the Sèvres porcelain factory.

The fabric designers were keen to see a free design school open in Lyon, and in 1757 their efforts to achieve this were rewarded: the Académie française established a school, directed by Donat Nonotte, the portrait painter, at which painting, sculpture, geometry and botany were taught. The designers also wanted the pupils to learn basic technology and economics.

Most designers had a speciality of their own, for example the decoration of watered silk, velvet or damask. Some were also able mechanics and worked at improving the performance of the loom so that their weaving would not be hindered by technical constraints. These constraints were, however, formidable: the Jacquard loom had not yet been invented and the looms designed by Falcon and Vaucanson, before Jacquard's great step forward, proved difficult to use. The problem was to raise the right warp threads to let the shuttle carrying the weft threads pass under them; the more complicated the design, the more necessary were the weaver's assistants whose job it was to raise the warp threads.[17] Other technical challenges included the re-use of patterns in new compositions in order to avoid having to re-thread the loom from the very beginning each time; the reduction of the amount of gold used on the back of a brocade in order not to waste silk; and the calculation of the number of colours, the special yarns required and the complexity of the weave in order not to go above the wholesale price of the fabric, fixed by the manufacturer.

This is why the ingenuity of the weavers, who produced so many different effects using such relatively simple means, arouses such astonishment. *Cannetillés* were produced by carrying warp threads over a specific number of weft threads; *lisérés* had wefts that were of various colours simultaneously, sometimes only two or three threads of each colour at a time, to give the impression of a very rich range of colours. This technique can be identified by horizontal stripes on the back of the fabric. The thickness of the threads can be varied, thick warp threads and thin weft threads or vice versa, or two warps and two wefts can be woven simultaneously, in different thicknesses and colours, one on the outside and one hidden away behind, the back one unobtrusive until brought to the top to create a pattern.

Brocades were obtained by using special shuttles that carried only the silk – or metal – through the warp when required. The more complicated the design on a piece of fabric the narrower the fabric, often only fifty centimetres wide, because it is impossible to increase the warp threads beyond a certain number. A few very wide pieces of silk, produced in Lyon at the request of Louis XV, are the magnificent exceptions that prove the rule. At the end of the reign of Louis XVI the small, multicoloured motifs decorating the stripes were produced by the 'trailing thread' technique, that is, using coloured warp threads that appeared only at specific points and floated loosely at the back when not wanted for the pattern. This piece of technical innovation was well adapted to the taste of the day, but also demonstrates some of the commercial difficulties that arose as the Revolution, set to stifle all luxury trades, approached.

Printing on Fabric

Another method of decorating fabric, besides weaving and embroidery, existed in eighteenth-century France. This was printing, invented long before in India and not known in Europe until the seventeenth century. In this century also the various East India companies – the Dutch, English and French – had begun importing to Europe printed cottons (fig. 23), called 'Indiennes', which were an instant success with the well-heeled and well-dressed. These imported cottons, however, were immediately accused of competing unfairly with traditional fabrics and were banned – in France for longer than elsewhere: it was not until 1759 that the authorities, tired of the way the obstinate French clientèle continued to procure the fabric illegally in spite of the restrictions, lifted the ban.

From that moment a new industry took hold in France, developed initially by foreigners of whom the most illustrious, Oberkampf, opened a factory in Jouy-en-Josas which soon began to supply the court, then the town, then the provinces. The Indian's secret, gradually penetrated by the French, consisted of printing fabrics with a block soaked in compounds based on mineral salts, then plunging the fabric into a dye bath. The compounds reacted with the dye to produce fast colour. Now, without too great an outlay, the populace could exchange their drab clothing for brightly coloured prints. Nevertheless, at the end of the eighteenth century Indiennes were still quite expensive and were available only to those enjoying a certain level of income. They did not really reach the working classes until the beginning of the nineteenth century.

In the eighteenth century silks were sometimes submitted to a dyeing process known as *chiné à la branche*. The warp threads were hermetically wrapped at places where they were required not to take the dye, and dipped into a dye bath. Then they were removed from the dye, wrapped again in different places and dipped a second time. This was repeated until all the chosen colours had been used. Finally they were woven with weft threds to give the effect of slightly smudged patterns. It was not until the nineteenth century that printing on the warp was used to obtain the same result.

Chapter Five

French Fashion and Fashion in Europe and the East

Exchanges with England

Throughout the eighteenth century France held sway as the cultural centre of Europe, and fashions worn there strongly influenced fashion in the other European countries. There was, however, competition, between France and England, England being the other great power (commercial and maritime in her case) in Europe, and as well equipped as France to influence the rest of the world. Before reviewing the relationship between costume in France and costume in the other countries in general, it is worth considering in some detail France's relations with her neighbour across the Channel.

The British aristocracy were pragmatists: they had a taste for the simple life, lived close to nature, enjoyed physical exercise and had a marked tendency towards austerity. At the end of the 1720s their clothing was less bulky, less fragile and more comfortable than that worn by members of the same social class in France, who were interested above all in appearances, for the sake of which they were prepared to endure almost any amount of discomfort.

As the increasing influence of England established itself amongst men and women of fashion in France, they began to develop a taste for the comfort of woollen clothing and for what today would be termed sports clothing – sport at that time being more or less restricted to riding. It was the horseman's riding coat which, during the reign of Louis XV, was the first garment to cross the Channel. Later, during the reign of Louis XVI, the tailcoat and the round hat, borrowed from the working classes by men of fashion (who were often accused at the time of dressing like coachmen), made the crossing as well. Thanks to the fashion plates of Gravelot, women in France were introduced to English hoops and the *mantua*, which, as discussed above, in France was called the *robe à l'anglaise*. On the eve of the Revolution, Frenchwomen also borrowed from England the fashion for somewhat masculine riding coats and for cotton muslin

26. Thomas Gainsborough, *Robert Andrews and his Wife, Frances*, *c.*1748–9. National Gallery, London.

tunics – which were worn also by small girls who, like the future Madame de Boigne, were happy to be able to play in comfort and with ease at last.[1]

Although England gave France its practical clothing, when the English wanted to dress up they were easily won over to the fashions of Paris – to the grave disapproval of certain patriots who would have liked Britain to rule the waves in every sphere, and who protested violently against this 'ridiculous imitation of the French'.[2] The French gown or *robe à la française* was nevertheless worn in England (where it was called the 'sack'), as was the *polonaise*, though both were sometimes modified a little to give them a local character. The English version of the French gown was sometimes completely closed down the front, or else it opened on to a quilted underskirt made of different fabric. The *polonaise* was worn over quite small hoops which looked almost flat over the hips and back. Amusingly, the *robe à l'anglaise* worn in France in a slightly modified version returned to its country of origin in about 1785 and was known there by its French name.[3]

Men's court and ceremonial clothing was of very similar cut in both countries. After about 1740 women's court clothing in England – worn only very occasionally it is true – was supported by immense, hideous rectangular paniers of a shape and size that were never imitated in France.[4] It is worth remembering, in fact, that although England gave the panier to France at the beginning of the eighteenth century, it had reached England from Germany, Germany having received it from Austria; Austria, in turn, was heir by royal marriage to Spain with its celebrated *guardinfante* (farthingale). The English, therefore, owed to their Hanoverian dynastic connections their gigantic appendages (previously scorned by those unwilling to wear anything so bulky).

Hats made by milliners or, in France, *modistes*, made their appearance in both countries simultaneously, which suggests that the idea must have been 'in the air' at the time. England, however, adopted the cashmere shawl before France, where it arrived only in the wake of Napoleon's campaign in Egypt.

Relations with the Holy Roman Empire

In Austria, where Spanish influence had been dominant at court until the accession of the Empress Maria-Theresa and her husband, François I of Lorraine, the growing fashion for French clothing was stimulated by the marriage of their daughter Marie-Antoinette to the future King Louis XVI. Maria-Theresa was an authoritarian monarch who, in imitation of Louis XIV and his personal livery, established a uniform consisting of a red wool suit and a gold-embroidered waistcoat for men and a gold and silver brocaded dress for women, which visitors to her castle at Laxembourg were obliged to wear. A police regulation relating to the dress to be worn by each of the (civil) classes of society successfully repressed any personal initiative.

In nearly all the small courts in Germany strict Spanish etiquette was combined with the imitation of French fashion. This led to all kinds of extravagances on the part of the Germans, who proved to be easy prey to unscrupulous tradesmen who would pass off 'scraps of fashion unheard of in the French capital' as the latest novelty from Paris. French dressmakers, meanwhile, criss-crossed the country seeking clients and, when the first German fashion magazines appeared in 1782 and 1787, advertized extensively, offering authentic French models. In the midst of this nationwide passion for elegance and opulence, Friedrich Wilhelm I of Prussia and his son Frederick the Great were the exceptions that proved the rule, both professing to despise fine clothes and fashion. Frederick the Great mocked the Count of Bruhl, the arbiter of fashion in Dresden, who boasted of owning fifteen hundred wigs, five hundred muffs and forty-seven furs; the

27. Watercolour by Ignaz Manzador (recto and verso), *The Empress Maria-Theresa of Austria in Mourning*, *c*.1770. Private collection.

Emperor declared that 'that was a lot [of wigs] for a man who has no head'.[5] On the other hand, he took a personal interest in the importing of sheep from Spain, the improvement of weaving techniques for woollen fabrics, the improvement of silk-weaving and the raising of silkworms. As a protectionist measure, he forbade the wearing of imported silk or lace in his presence, as well as the wearing of Indian cotton prints. The importation of printed cotton from India was banned in Leipzig until 1750.

Relations with Spain, Portugal and Italy

Fashionable society in all three countries, Spain, Portugal and Italy, generally followed French fashion in its broad outlines, although variations of detail were introduced that bore witness (to varying degrees) to the survival of national traditions.

In Spain the royal family was of French origin, and the influence of Paris was discernible at court. Goya's elegant beauties, however, with their shorter dresses, shawls and mantillas held in place by large tortoiseshell combs, and his men strapped tightly into their costumes, bound by a broad belt, are typically Spanish.

28. Francisco Goya, *The Countess of Carpilo, Duchess of Solona*, *c*.1794. Musée du Louvre, Paris.

In Portugal the court favoured French art and dressed according to the 'fashions of Paris'[6] – as far as elegant clothing was concerned: as was noted above, King John v ordered an entire wardrobe from Paris in 1735. Nevertheless, the women continued to wear bodices with basques, a throwback to the Spanish *basquine* of the seventeenth century.

The Italians adapted French costume to suit their taste for Baroque ornamentation, weighing their clothes down with the heavy, sinuous bands of gold embroidery that made masculine dress of the period

29. Pietro Longhi, *The Sagredo Family*, *c.*1752. Galleria Querini Stampaglia, Venice.

particularly dazzling, and accentuating the curves on feminine gowns with puffed sleeves. In Italy, as everywhere else, it was the well-dressed city dwellers who were caught up in the current of fashions from France. In the provinces regional variations, many of them dating back to the fifteenth century, were retained.

Relations with the Low Countries, Switzerland and the Scandinavian Countries

In the Low Countries and Switzerland the influence of a court was absent. These countries spoke French and loved the French language, and although theirs was a bourgeois society their taste for elegance naturally led them in the direction of France. Nevertheless these were the countries where English and French fashions were most likely to be found in co-existence, mingled with the traditional costume that remained very popular outside the towns, especially in the valleys of Switzerland.

Denmark and Sweden, although further from Paris, enjoyed old-established links with the French capital, forged by the French artists who had worked in Scandinavia in the seventeenth century.

Royal portraits in the Scandinavian countries demonstrate the persistence of very exaggerated paniers of the Spanish type. Some of the men's clothing in the costume collections of the Castle of Christianborg in Copenhagen[7] and the Royal Armoury in Stockholm was ordered in Paris and owes most of its features to French fashion. In spite of this, in 1778 King Gustav III tried to impose a standard national costume on his courtiers: it consisted of various outdated features of sixteenth-century dress (slashed sleeves, puffed breeches, ruffs, strait-lacing) – an indication of nascent romanticism.

Relations with Eastern Europe

In Poland, the taste for things French, introduced in the seventeenth century by Queen Maria-Luisa de Gonzaga, who was French, grew more pronounced during the reign of the last king of Poland, Stanislas-August Poniatowski (1764–1795); as Madame Geoffrin noted during her travels along the Vistula, the court made every effort to copy French fashion. The provincial aristocracy, however, pre-

30. Anonymous, *Catherine II in the Ceremonial Dress of the Order of St Catherine.* Private collection. The empress is wearing court dress in the French style.

ferred a costume that was Hungarian in influence, called a *sarmate*, and the townspeople and peasants were loyal to their traditional garb of a *zoupane* (an underdress) and *contouche* (an overdress with slashed sleeves, similar to the *robe à la française*); in fact, for reasons unknown, *contouche* was the name given in Germany to the *robe à la française*.

The *polonaise* was only symbolically related to the country whose name it bore. Poland was, in fact, content to absorb the influence of France, without giving anything in exchange.

31. Jean-Baptiste Le Prince, *The Russian Baptism*, 1765. Musée du Louvre, Paris.

The Europeanisation of Russia had been one of the ambitions of Peter the Great, and it was carried further by his daughter, the Tsarina Elizabeth, who introduced French fashion to court. Elizabeth was very stylish and interested on a very grand scale in clothes, all of which she had made in Paris. It appears that, at her death in 1761, there were fifteen thousand gowns in her wardrobe, plus thousands of pairs of slippers and mules. Her example of adopting French fashion may have been followed by the aristocracy, but members of the other classes of Russian society retained their traditional dress, which was oriental in influence. A French artist, Jean-Baptiste Le Prince, made sketches of traditional clothes while on a trip to Russia in the middle of the century, thereby contributing to the introduction of oriental styles into France.

* * *

The Influence of the Orient

The French taste for oriental dress lasted right through the eighteenth century. It was originally inspired by the picturesque ceremonial surrounding visits to court by the Sultan's envoys in their national dress, and by the clothes worn by certain ambassadors' wives on their return from postings in the Levant; in addition, there were the portraits in the Turkish style by Aved and Liotard, and, finally, a very strong influence – there were plays full of characters from the harem – like Favart's *The Three Sultans*. Oriental costume was soft and comfortable to wear compared with current European fashions, and this is what women were beginning to want.

Initially, oriental costume was worn only as fancy dress, or for theatricals. Madame de Pompadour wore it in her theatre, and as a souvenir of her performances she commissioned Carl van Loo to paint a series of portraits of her in seraglio dress for her Château de Bellevue. Oriental dress was worn at home, informally, but it took longer for it to achieve the status of serious clothing, which was achieved by the sporadic introduction of details – often simply a shape – borrowed from the traditional costume of the vast region that stretched from Poland to Turkey and embraced Russia. The general characteristic of the clothes was a draped, fluid outline.

From 1775 a succession of oriental styles passed through the wardrobes of French ladies of fashion: the *polonaise*, the *lévite*, the *circassian*, as well as the Turkish, the sultana and the levantine gowns. The *polonaise* was borrowed from Poland in name alone; the *lévite* became fashionable after a production of Racine's tragedy *Athalie* at the Comédie Française in which members of the tribe of Levi were clothed in an adaptation of a Middle Eastern style. The *circassian* and Turkish gowns, on the other hand, featured layered sleeves of different lengths which were borrowed from genuinely oriental clothing.

Turkish dresses, when worn without a panier, bore a striking resemblance to the dresses worn in paintings by Le Prince, particularly *The Russian Baptism*, exhibited in the Salon of 1765 (fig. 31). In 1779 the *Galerie des Modes et Costumes français* published a *robe à la levantine* which was alleged to have been the creation of one Sarrazin, a theatrical costumier; it is, however, an exact copy of the gown worn by the woman holding a candle in the painting by Le Prince. Over a long-sleeved gown, the woman wears a sort of pelisse with short sleeves, open in front, slightly waisted at the back, falling to a point at either side and bordered all round with fur. It was, therefore, thanks to the theatre, that an authentic Russian garment was made available to women. Others were made public through portraits of actresses in oriental costume, such as the portrait of Sophie Arnould by Greuze, now in the Los Angeles County Museum of Art. With their fluid lines, their soft drapery crossing over the chest without squeezing it, their loosely belted waists, these gowns prepared the way for a new style: the Directoire.

Part Two

Chapter Six

Clothes for Special Occasions

So far in this survey, the evolution of clothes worn on a day-to-day basis throughout the eighteenth century has been discussed. However, how did people dress at different times of the year, or for physical recreation such as riding, or for amusements such as dancing? And what did they wear for important occasions such as a baptism, first communion, marriage, mourning – occasions that were accompanied by a certain amount of ceremony, at which clothing had its role to play?

Seasonal Variations

Men and women of fashion wore different materials at different times of the year: taffetas, muslins and bobbin lace in summer; satin, velvet and needle lace in winter. There was no particular difference in the clothes themselves, the styles remaining generally the same.

Winter clothing was fairly specific. Men wore waistcoats with long sleeves; the waistcoats were backed with woollen fabric and lined with silk or plush. During the reign of Louis XVI the old and frail used sometimes to wear two sets of clothes, one on top of the other. Fur was used more for decoration (around the collar or the edges) than for comfort. At the beginning of Louis XVI's reign, however, women had little palatines made for themselves, like the one so beloved of the sister-in-law of Louis XIV. They also wore calf-length capes, called *pelisses*, lined with fur. The accessory that came best to symbolise winter was the muff: during the reign of Louis XV, women used to carry small muffs made of fur; on the eve of the Revolution, men and women alike carried large muffs made from a variety of materials.

* * *

32. Carle Van Loo, *The Hunting Party at Rest*, 1737. Musée du Louvre, Paris.

Riding Habits

The only sports practised in France during the eighteenth century were riding and hunting. Apart from the brightly coloured uniform with its gold braid worn by the hunt, there was no special clothing for men. In bad weather boots and the *redingote* (from the English 'riding coat') were the mark of the huntsman. However, by the latter part of the century, under Louis XVI, the passion for English clothing and a tendency towards more functional wear combined to produce a short, fitted riding jacket for horse racing or hunting; this had a kind of cuff round the lower hem in imitation of military costume, and was worn with leather breeches.

Women rode side-saddle and wore a long skirt with a jacket to just below hip level, or a full-length riding coat more or less modelled on the men's *redingote*. In Carle van Loo's *Halte de Chasse* (*The Hunting Party at Rest*; fig. 32), painted in 1737, the women are shown wearing long coats with braided motifs down the front edges and worn open at the front, over a bodice and skirt. These coats have a wide belt and elbow-length sleeves with broad cuffs like those on the men's coats. A three-cornered hat, smaller and flatter than the men's version, completes the outfit.

A special whale-boned bodice with a short front was designed at this period 'for women who ride on horseback'.[1] During the reign of Louis XVI both garments, the jacket and the riding coat, were still in use. A painting by Moreau le Jeune, *Rencontre au Bois de Boulogne* (*Meeting in the Bois de Boulogne*), shows a jacket with turned-back edges like the men's version. The *Galerie des Modes et Costumes français* published an illustration of a *caraco* with buttoned lapels, very tight-waisted with a full basque; it showed also *redingotes* with lapels and large buttons. A big, plumed hat was the indispensable accompaniment to these outfits.

Women on horseback wore also long tight underpants beneath their skirts: these were usually of black knitted silk, like the ones mentioned in the posthumous inventory of Madame de Pompadour. Louis-Auguste Brun painted a portrait of Marie-Antoinette (whose mother reproached her for being too bold) dressed for riding, wearing a pair of tight breeches decorated with braid and embroidery. The audacity of Marie-Antoinette's dress is emphasised by the fact that the *Galerie des Modes*, inspired by Brun's painting to publish a print of the outfit, replaced the queen's breeches with a traditional riding skirt.[2]

Masked Balls

Masked balls had their own specific garment, the domino, a long, full silk gown with a hood which covered the clothes beneath completely. It was worn by both men and women when they did not want to wear fancy-dress, or if they wished to go dancing incognito. Jean-Marc Nattier portrayed the marquise de la Ferté-Imbault, daughter of Madame Geoffrin, wearing a domino in 1740. In 1742, Maurice Quentin de La Tour drew a pastel portrait of the presidente de Rieux (now in the Musée Cognacq-Jay) wearing the same garb. Moreau le Jeune's plate showing Louis XVI, similarly cloaked, at a ball at the Hôtel de Ville in 1782, demonstrates the persistence of a traditional garment which in fact survived well into the nineteenth century, although it was later worn more by men than by women.

33. Engraving by Janninet, after Leclerc, *Galerie des Modes et Costumes français* (reprinted by P. Cornu, plate 170). A woman dressed in a domino on her way to a masked ball.

Baptism

During the reign of Louis XV, babies were seldom formally baptised at birth. The custom, at both ends of the social scale, was to give new-born babies a private and rapid baptism, and then to defer the official ceremony until much later, often until the age of first communion or even just before marriage.

The children of Louis XV, Mesdames the First and Second (twin sisters), Madame the Third (born fourth, but the third child had died) and Monseigneur le Dauphin, whose respective dates of birth were 1727, 1732 and 1729, were not baptised until 1737, in the chapel at the Château de Versailles, where they received their first names, Louise-Elisabeth, Anne-Henriette, Marie-Adelaide and Louis. Although this was not a court ceremony, the young prince wore a suit of silver brocade with openings at the places where he would receive the holy oil. The three little princesses each wore a child's dress with dangling sleeves, made of silver watered silk.[3] The only special baptismal apparel worn on that day was the *chrémeau* or *toquet*, a small lace cap symbolising childhood and innocence, placed on the child's head after the anointment with oil.

Under Louis XVI the tradition was reversed, and a greater number of children, including royal children, were officially baptised at birth.

The baby's layette at the time was all white, so it was easy to respect the colour symbolism.

First Communion

The earliest first communion took place in France in 1593. The ceremony was described for the first time in 1616, and by the eighteenth century it was standard practice.

For most children it appears that no special clothing was required. At the beginning of the seventeenth century first communicants were enjoined to wash their face and hands and to wear their best clothes; 'bare throats' for girls were condemned by Père Laurent Chifflet of the Society of Jesus.[4] The same prescriptions applied in the eighteenth century, when children would be fitted out with new clothing for their first communion. There were charities to help families that could not afford such expense: we know from their records what kind of clothes were worn. Between 1771 and 1783, in Coutances, in Normandy, the charity that clothed poor children for their first communion used to provide girls with a camisole of white drugget, a skirt of white dimity, a striped silk and cotton apron, a headdress and coif of light coloured linen, a muslin handkerchief, and clogs with sheepskin linings. Boys received a suit of brown drugget with 'partridge eye' dimity breeches with buckled garters, and clogs.[5]

Some first communions were held in the parish church, particularly in towns; in country districts, in many cases, no first communions were celebrated until after the Restoration in 1814. Secondary schools, colleges and religious foundations were also the location for first-communion ceremonies. For boys in secondary schools no special uniform seems to have been required. Things were different in girls' convents; the upper classes considered it desirable to send their daughters to a convent for a year or two around the time of their first communion – the preparation for which was seen as the main function of convents. As a way of appealing to the emotions of the children in their care, the Ursulines introduced the white dress (a symbol of innocence and purity) in the early seventeenth century. By the eighteenth century the white linen gown and headdress, plus the white taffeta sash, were obligatory with the Ursulines.[6] The fashion spread to other orders and in sophisticated convents was often much more extravagant – white silk embroidered with silver, for example.

The communion dress of Hélène Massalska, the future princesse de Ligne, in the Abbaye-aux-Bois, was in silver-striped watered silk. Nine days after the ceremony, before leaving the class set up to prepare girls for their first communion and abandoning the white ribbons that were the insignia of the class, she and her classmates made an offering of their dresses to the sacristy.[7] Towards the end of the century, Saint-Sulpice added a veil to the outfit in order to dissuade the girls from spending so many hours in front of the mirror arranging their hair on the morning of the ceremony.[8]

At Versailles, first communion and confirmation provided the occasion for the royal princesses of France to wear their first court gown. These gowns were very constricting for the young girls.

Marriage

In the eighteenth century marriage was a matter of proprieties and interests rather than of feelings, particularly amongst the aristocracy. It was almost always arranged by the family – like the one arranged for Mademoiselle Houdetot (as recounted by Madame d'Epinay) in the space of an evening. François Bluche noted amusingly that marriages were entered into between the ages of thirteen and ninety years old.[9] Where the age gap was disproportionate it was usually the husband-to-be who was the older and the fiancée much younger, but marriages between children were not unheard of. Some of them separated as soon as the ceremony was over, madame going back to the convent for a while and monsieur travelling with a tutor. The average age for marriage, however, was between sixteen and twenty.

Whatever the age of the couple, they had to be dressed appropriately for the ceremony. Amongst the lower middle classes the wedding clothes were recorded in the marriage contract and often constituted the main components of the dowry. Even if she were only thirteen years old, the bride had to be dressed in an off-the-shoulder gown, with her hair dressed and her make-up (including beauty spots[10]) in place, exactly like a miniature adult. Her dress would be exceedingly lavish, and coloured. Baroness d'Oberkirch recalled 'the gown of flame-coloured grogram' worn by Madame Hendel, the housekeeper at the Château de Montbéliard, to receive her young mistress, bride of the comte du Nord. This dress – 'so dazzling that the Grand-Duke asked her if it were not a gown for an auto-da-fé' –

34. Engraving by Dupin, after Leclerc, *Galerie des Modes et Costumes français* (reprinted by P. Cornu, plate 88). Young bride being led up to the altar, 1779.

had been her wedding dress and was fetched from the chest only for the most solemn occasions.[11] A coloured fashion plate of 1779 shows 'a young bride being led to the altar, wearing a gown of Chinese silk' trimmed with gauze, ribbons and flowers. Another plate of the same date figures a 'woman in ceremonial gown on the day of her marriage.'[12] The outfit is vivid red.

At about this time, however, some young women were beginning to prefer a white dress. On 1 April 1776 Henriette-Louise de Waldner de Freudstein was 'all dressed up, with plenty of lace *à l'anglaise*', wearing 'a gown of rose-point over an underskirt of white *dauphine*' for her marriage to Monsieur d'Oberkirch, who himself was 'most elegantly turned out in a suit of light-blue silk embroidered in gold.'[13] In 1787 the seventeen-year-old Henriette-Lucy Dillon, the future marquise de la Tour du Pin, was married in a 'gown of white crape, beautifully trimmed with Brussels lace, with lace bands hanging from her headdress'. At that time a cap was worn but no veil; a wreath of orange was worn on the head and a bouquet carried in the hand. The marquise's *Mémoires* continue: 'For the wedding breakfast I wore a beautiful hat decorated with white feathers and with the orange-blossom bouquet attached to it.'[14] In *Le Mariage de Figaro*,

Beaumarchais dresses Suzanne and Marceline in the same kind of hat, known as a 'bride's hat'.

The custom of wearing a white wedding dress with a long veil did not really become established until the beginning of the nineteenth century, but Madame de la Tour du Pin mentions that for the signing of the marriage contract she wore either a pink or a blue dress[15] (her memory is a trifle shaky), colours that were later very popular with young girls for the same ceremony. She mentions also the somewhat extravagant habit of giving presents to all the guests – sword-knots, fans, hat ribbons, belt tassels, etc.[16]

Mourning

In his *Tableau de Paris*, Sébastien Mercier wrote,

> Court mourning saves the good people of Paris a lot of money . . . Black clothing goes wonderfully well with mud, bad weather, economy and their dislike of spending time on their toilette! A poet of my acquaintance cried out, 'I have received a legacy from the King.' 'What? How?' 'How? I would have spent twenty *pistoles* on an outfit this spring, but I can put the money back in my pocket. I shall willingly wear mourning for so generous a sovereign.[17]

Fabric merchants were less satisfied, however, when their rich materials, woven at great expense, unexpectedly became unsaleable. Royal and court mourning (fig. 27) was worn by the whole nation at that period, and for six months all colour and jewellery were put aside; the royal household provided mourning for everyone directly employed by the Crown. The length of the mourning period, whether court or individual, was 'one of the principle reasons for shops to close and manufacture to cease'. A court order of 3 June 1716 reduced the mourning period by a half. The etiquette of mourning was not simplified at all, however, and this encouraged the creation of a special newspaper, the *Annonce des deuils*, indicating 'the day the mourning begins, how long it lasts and the form that it should take.'[18]

A few years before the Revolution, full mourning dress – that is, mourning divided into three successive stages: wool, silk and half-mourning – was worn only for a father, mother, husband or wife,

35. Engraving by Dupin, after Leclerc, *Galerie des Modes et Costumes français* (original edition, plate 211). Full court mourning, 1781.

brother, sister and cousin. Mourning for less close relations was divided into two stages only: black and white, and the women were permitted to wear diamonds and men to carry a sword and wear silver buckles on their shoes.

'Mourning for a mother or father lasts six months. During the first three months wool is worn, either poplin or *raz de Saint-Maur*, trimmed with plain fringes;[19] stockings and gloves in black silk; bronze shoes and buckles.' When in full court dress women wore 'caps in fine black muslin, flat lappets trimmed with plain fringes, long headdresses, mantillas of the same material and white crape sleeves'. With their street dress they would wear 'caps, lappets, sleeves and fichus in white crape with plain fringes . . . . After six weeks the head-dress is put aside, ruffled lappets and black jewellery may be worn. When three months have passed, black silk is worn for six weeks, silk velvet in the winter, taffeta from Tours in the summer; headdress, sleeves and fichu are of brocaded gauze trimmed with cut fringes. The final six weeks are in half-mourning. White is worn, with brocaded gauze (also for the accessories), and diamonds.'

Mourning for a grandfather or grandmother lasted for only four and a half months: six weeks in wool, six in silk and six in half-mourning. For a brother or sister, six weeks was sufficient (three in wool, two in silk, one in half-mourning); three weeks for uncles and aunts (all in silk, a fortnight with fringes, a week with brocaded or pale-coloured gauze); two weeks for second cousins (a week with fringes, a week in brocaded gauze); eleven days for a father or mother's first cousin (six in black, five in white) and eight days for the children of second cousins (five in black, three in white).

The mourning period for a husband was longer: a year and six weeks. For the first six months widows wore 'a *raz de Saint-Maur*[20] gown with a long train that could be pulled up using a cord attached to the side of the petticoat, drawn through the pocket; no pleats either at the front or the back, and the two halves of the front fastened by hooks or ribbons; no *compères*; funnel-shaped sleeves, a cambric headdress with broad hems, a fine cambric fichu, a black crape belt fastened in front, its two ends reaching down to the hem; a crape stole pleated at the back, a large black crape hat, gloves, shoes and shoe buckles of bronze, a muff covered in *raz de Saint-Maur*, untrimmed, or a crape fan'. During the second six months widows wore 'black silk, with sleeves and trimmings of white crape and black jewellery, if they so wished'. The final six weeks were the plain black and white weeks, with a headdress and sleeves of brocaded gauze and accessories in either black or white.

Mourning for a wife lasted for only six months. Widows were not allowed to appear at court until the end of the first six months, but widowers could return after a few days. They had to wear a woollen coat and hose, cambric cuffs with a flat hem, bronze sword, shoes and buckles, a plain cravat, large *pleureuses* (bands of white linen or cambric around the coat cuffs); after the first three weeks, small *pleureuses* could be worn. 'After six weeks, stockings could be of black silk and the cuffs fringed, but the sword and buckles had to remain black. During the following six weeks, the coat was of black silk and the sword and buckles of silver.' During the last six weeks, when half-mourning was worn, the stockings were of white silk.

The mourning period for relatives from whom one inherited money or property was six months, the same as for a father or mother; people of title or rank also mourned the death of the head of the family for six months, even when they were quite distant cousins.

The king wore purple for mourning and the queen white, but they did not go into mourning for royal children who died below the age of seven. The chancellor, supreme head of justice and the embodiment of its impartiality, was the only person in the country never to wear mourning at all.

Chapter Seven

Etiquette and Uniforms

No comprehensive description of the clothes worn by French society in the eighteenth century could neglect the official ceremonial dress worn by the king and his courtiers, particularly as this dress was linked directly to the institutions of the country. At this period, the king was still the keystone of the structure that was France, monarch by divine right, and, indeed, almost the object of worship; the court ceremonial established by Henri III and elaborated upon by Louis XIV revolved entirely around him. The clothes worn by him for the solemn enactment of his duties, and the clothes imposed on his entourage by etiquette, were imbued with symbolism relating to the personage of the king.

The clothes worn by the king defined him externally as the representative of France, responsible at times for various duties of a semi-religious nature, such as being the protector or grand master of the orders of chivalry. His clothes also constituted the vestments of the cult surrounding him and defined the people who were at his service – those in charge of his protection or comfort, or responsible for organising his distractions.

The Representative of France

Official portraits of the king, following the particularly felicitous example set by Rigaud in his portrait of Louis XIV, the Sun King, show the sovereign in majesty, surrounded by the insignia of his royal status – crown, sceptre, the hand of justice – and wearing clothes from a different age – the white clothes of the Knights of the Holy Spirit, fossilised by tradition in the fashion of the sixteenth century, when the order was created. The white suit is covered by the great royal cloak of blue with gold fleurs-de-lis (like the French coat of arms) and lined with ermine whose cut dated back to the Middle Ages. The chain of the order of which the king was the grand master can be seen

36. The first robe worn by the king at his coronation. Engraving from *Le Sacre et couronnement de Louis XVI* (detail), Paris, 1775.

glinting on the ermine draped over his left shoulder. The clothes signify that the person wearing them is the embodiment of France in all aspects, the avowed defender of his country, around whom the Order of the Holy Spirit revolved. Rigaud painted the young Louis XV in the same dress in 1716, when he was only six years old and had not yet been crowned. The legitimacy and authority of the young king, sometimes called into question during his regency, were thus proclaimed in advance.

The Lord's Anointed

The coronation ceremony made the king the Lord's anointed, holder of temporal power and, by God's will, a personage midway between lay society and the Church, to whom his subjects owed obedience and respect. Although a coronation is not technically a sacrament, the position of the king as the Lord's anointed explains the religious significance of the clothing worn by the sovereign for the ceremony.[1]

On 25 October 1722, at the age of twelve (the age at which members of the royal family attained their majority), Louis XV crossed the threshold of Reims cathedral dressed in a full-length robe of cloth of silver. This silver robe was replaced in due course by a *camisole*, a sort of long-sleeved cassock in crimson satin, trimmed with gold braid and open (as was the shirt worn under it) at the places where the new king would be anointed with oil from the Holy Ampulla. On 11 June 1775, identically dressed, Louis XVI, aged twenty-one, also entered Reims cathedral. Once the unction had been performed, the openings in the clothes were closed, and the king put on a pair of velvet boots, then a tunic and a dalmatic, corresponding to the robes of a deacon and a sub-deacon, and finally the great royal mantle, which took the place of the priest's chasuble. All the layers were embroidered with gold fleurs-de-lis. Since the coronation of Louis XIII the mantle had changed colour, from blue to purple. Jean-Pierre Bayard wrote that purple was the royal colour *par excellence*, because it was a compromise between the azure of the French coat of arms and the fiery red of the cardinals' robes and therefore emphasised the twin powers, temporal and religious.[2] The mantle had a long train and, like the thirteenth-century *garnache*, opened to the right. It was fastened on the shoulder by a lozenge-shaped jewel bearing a fleur-de-lis and precious stones – diamonds and pearls. The left side was carried over the arm. The shape had remained unchanged since the Middle Ages; only the colour had changed.

The King Acclaimed by his Vassals

Before the anointing took place, the king-to-be swore the oath of allegiance to his country, to the Order of the Holy Spirit and to the military Order of Saint-Louis. The sword, gloves and ring were blessed, then finally the sceptre and the hand of justice were handed to the king.

The coronation took place after the anointing, with the crown known as Charlemagne's crown, a simple circle with a large ruby set in the front. At the end of the ceremony the archbishop of Reims replaced the Charlemagne crown with a smaller, lighter one. The crown of Louis XV was the only one to escape destruction in the French Revolution. It was ornamented with two famous diamonds, the Sancy and the Regent, later replaced by imitations.

The next stage, the king's enthronement and acclaim by twelve peers – six ecclesiastical and six lay – was a reminder of the time when the monarchy had been elected. The lay peers were clothed in calf-length robes in cloth of gold, cut like cassocks, with violet, gold and silver silk girdles, and cloaks with trains in purple wool, open in front at the centre, with ermine linings and a short ermine cloak (*épitoge*) over the left shoulder. Each wore a count's coronet on his head.

For every stage of the coronation – the swearing of the oath, the anointment, the coronation and the enthronement – costumes dating back to the Middle Ages were worn, and these had kept something of their original religious character. The same tradition applied to the costumes of the grand officers of the Crown, the grand master of the king's house, the grand chamberlain, the first gentleman of the bed chamber and the grand master of the wardrobe; all were dressed like the lay peers. Also in medieval clothing was the lord chancellor and keeper of the seals, robed in the same way as all other members of the legal profession. In the royal procession he wore a cassock of crimson satin and a full-length cloak of scarlet wool, similar in style to the king's cloak. It was lined and bordered with ermine and the left shoulder was also draped with ermine; on his head he wore a judge's flat-topped cap in cloth of gold, edged with ermine.

Court Ceremonial

There was another, quite different type of costume rubbing shoulders with these medieval costumes at court. This was worn by courtiers whose function was largely ceremonial – heralds-at-arms, Swiss guards, the master and grand master of ceremonies, ushers of the king's bedchamber. The list recalls the enormously increased importance given to court ceremonial by Henri III, who in 1585 created the position of grand master of ceremonies. The trunk-hose and short cloak were retained from that period; the heralds-at-arms, however, replaced the latter with a purple tabard embroidered with gold fleurs-de-lis.

Finally, the prince carrying the royal train, the four lords guardian of the Holy Ampulla and the captain of the Scots guards were clothed in an extravagant version of the fashion of the day: a velvet suit trimmed with gold, plus a short cape with a collar, lined with cloth of gold. This uniform was also worn later at the coronation of Napoleon I.

★ ★ ★

The Grand Master and Protector of the Orders of Chivalry

THE ORDER OF THE HOLY SPIRIT

The day after the coronation in Reims cathedral, the king presided over a chapter of the Order of Knights of the Holy Spirit, whose grand master he had just become. The order was founded in December 1578 by Henri III, in memory of his accession to the throne one Whit Sunday. It was created as an attempt to attach the principal Catholic leaders to the royal cause, in the middle of the Wars of Religion. The chapter consisted of one hundred members: eighty-seven noble knights who were also members of the order of Saint-Michel (created by Louis XI and reformed by Louis XIV), nine ecclesiastical members and four grand officers or administrators, assisted by a varying number of lesser officers. To be appointed a knight, the candidate had to be at least thirty years old; princes of the blood were received at the time of their first communion and royal princes at birth.[3]

Novices wore the doublet and hose in cloth of silver (a symbol of purity) and the same bands in *point d'Angleterre* as those worn by the knights. On their head they wore a black hat trimmed with a small bunch of white feathers and a mass of heron feathers, and on their shoulders the *capot*, a small black velvet cape. On the day the novices took their oath the king replaced the small *capot* with the great cloak of the order. This cloak, cut in exactly the same fashion as the king's great coronation mantle, was in black velvet lined with orange-red satin, with a cape round the neck in fresh-green watered silk (in the Middle Ages this green was the colour worn by newly dubbed knights) and silver. Pentecostal flames embroidered in gold were scattered over the cloak; on the borders and round the neck were trophies and crowns in gold, with the letter H and fleurs-de-lis in silver. In the middle of the front a badge embroidered in silver bearing the eight-pointed gold cross with the gleaming dove in the centre was worn hanging from the collar. The designs on the collar were also embroidered round the edge of the cape. Senior officers – the provost, the treasurer, the secretary, the chancellor – wore the cloak without the cape; only the chancellor's cloak was embroidered with motifs borrowed from the designs on the collar. Commanders of the order wore neither cloak nor collar; they wore the cross of the order embroidered in silver on the left side of the scarlet and purple cloaks

37. François-Hubert Drouais, *The Comte de Provence, the Future Louis XVIII*. Musée du Château, Versailles. The great cloak of the Order of the Holy Spirit, in black velvet embroidered with gold.

worn by cardinals and prelates. The usher and the herald had great cloaks in black satin with capes of fresh green, fringed in gold and embroidered with gold flames.[4]

This was the ceremonial dress worn for the annual chapter of the Order on 1 January, for the ceremonies of 2 January, 2 February and for Pentecost. It was extremely expensive to buy, particularly the great cloak; the duc de Croÿ paid eight thousand pounds for his in 1775, consoling himself for the huge expense by reminding himself, in his memoirs, that 'It is an item of furniture which will remain in the family.' In fact, the cloaks were sometimes handed down from father to son, even over several generations; Mathieu Marais commented, after the ceremony of 1724, 'some fine new cloaks can be seen, but some very old ones as well'.

The whole outfit was very uncomfortable to wear and the cloak itself was extremely heavy. At the coronation of Louis XV the knights who, contrary to the usual custom, wore their cloaks for the offertory, got tangled up in their trains and 'nearly lost their lives'. For the order's usual ceremonies they wore short cloaks of black velvet and a jerkin of the same fabric, with the badge on the left side; the medal hung from a blue cord worn like a chain. As the years passed the less elaborate costume was worn more often, the huge ceremonial cloak eventually being abandoned, 'except by novices on the day of their reception'. Nevertheless, Louis XVI wore it for his coronation, but when he returned to his apartments after the ceremony he was 'jumping for joy at being rid of all that'. After the same ceremony the duc de Croÿ suffered from aching shoulders for two days.

On 1 January 1778 a new, more comfortable uniform came into use. This consisted of a 'black velvet suit . . . with facings embroidered in gold on green silk; the waistcoat, collar and lapels of the short black cape worn over the suit were also gold on green. For the ceremonial at Pentecost the velvet was replaced by a black *musulmane*. The hat was black, with white feathers. The hose were white'. This new uniform, 'extremely handsome and very expensive', as the duc de Croÿ noted, 'cost each knight one hundred *louis*'. As was the custom, the officers' clothes were plainer: a suit and cloak with no facings, a hat with no feathers.

The knights also had mourning clothes to wear at services for the dead. These consisted of a cloak and cape in black wool, with plain bands and linen, and a hat without feathers. The king, who always wore purple for mourning, would wear a large purple cloak.

THE ORDER OF SAINT-LAZARE AND MONT-CARMEL

The Orders of Saint-Michel and Saint-Louis had no uniform. The Order of Saint-Lazare and Mont-Carmel (a fusion of two institutions), on the other hand, had its own uniform which had been updated by the marquis de Dangeau, named grand master of the order by Louis XIV in 1693. The new costume was first worn on 17 December 1701, for the feast of St Lazarus. The grand master and the lay knights wore a *soubreveste* (a kind of knee-length dalmatic) in silver watered silk under a great cloak with a train, open in front, in amaranth velvet (the colour of Notre Dame du Mont-Carmel) lined in green satin (the colour of St Lazarus). The grand master's cloak was trimmed with gold embroidery and had a longer train than the knights' cloaks. The badge, worn on a broad amaranth ribbon like a pendant on the left hand side of the cloak, was also embroidered in silk and gold thread. Novices wore amaranth breeches and hose, plus shoes and a hat in the same colour; over their *soubreveste* they wore only a short, green satin cape lined with taffeta. The lay brothers wore a woollen *soubreveste* and unlined cloak, which hung four inches from the ground and was trimmed with pale pink silk. The ecclesiastical knights wore a cassock of amaranth watered silk, and a cappa magna (short cape) of the same fabric, lined in green satin; a cross was embroidered in silk and gold thread on the left sleeve. The usher was in a jerkin of amaranth wool. The herald's surcoat was in amaranth velvet, lined with green satin, embroidered in gold with a cartouche bearing the arms of the order. His hat bore a black aigrette with one amaranth and one green feather.

In 1778 this costume followed the general trend towards simpler clothing and became all black. The new uniform was a coat *à la française* with a short cloak, velvet in winter and grogram in summer, lined with crimson satin or silk twill; the waistcoat, lapels and collar of the cloak were all crimson, embroidered to a set pattern. The gold coat buttons were the uniform buttons of the order of Saint-Lazare. The badge of the order was stitched to the left side of the cloak. A cross on a green ribbon was worn between the suit and the cloak. The black silk breeches contrasted sharply with the white stockings. The black hat worn over undressed hair was trimmed in ducal fashion: two rows of white feathers speckled with crimson and a crimson grogram bow.[5] The sketch made by Madame Labille-Guyard for a painting that unfortunately no longer exists shows the reception of a knight in 1788; it suggests, in fact, that the suit in cloth of silver was still being worn.[6]

Official Ceremonies

A wedding was another occasion at which the king and the royal princes had to wear traditional costume, including, this time, the celebrated trunk hose of the sixteenth century, always made of some extravagant fabric. The all-black worn by Louis XIV for his marriage to Marie-Thérèse of Spain was abandoned at weddings in the eighteenth century in favour of gold and silver. When Louis XV married Marie Leczinska in the Château de Fontainebleau he wore a suit of gold brocade, embroidered in gold and with diamond buttons. The short cape that he chose instead of a cloak was made of gold Spanish lace.[7] For his first marriage, in 1745, his son wore cloth of gold with a large pattern of foliage on it, including the jacket, trunk hose and cloak; the trimmings were in gold lace, enriched with the most valuable pearls from the crown.[8] In 1770 the future King Louis XVI also wore a suit of cloth of gold which cost 12,322 *livres*.

Young royal brides wore clothes that resembled current court dress more than traditional costume, since the bride's gown had enormous paniers. Marie Leczinska, who became reigning queen on her marriage, had the right to wear the royal skirt (*jupe*) and cloak of purple velvet edged with ermine and sprigged with gold fleurs-de-lis. Her skirt was studded with jewels, her whalebone bodice fastened with diamond clasps. The cloak measured nine ells. Marie-Thérèse in 1745 and Marie-Antoinette in 1770 were marrying heirs apparent only and therefore had to make do with cloth of silver – albeit with a long train and trimmed with gold filigree.[9]

In fact, the grand ceremonial costumes were not used very frequently at court. The king never wore his coronation robes a second time, even at solemn sittings of parliament, which were the only occasions when he sat on his throne. At such formal occasions he wore a 'purple suit and cloak, trimmed with broad bands of embroidery, and wore a plumed hat on his head'.[10]

Court duties did not necessitate the wearing of uniform except on coronation day, although the grand master of ceremonies did wear a cloak of the same colour as his suit and carried a small baton, covered in black velvet, with an ivory knob.[11]

* * *

38. Uniform of a page of the king's bedchamber. Engraving from *Le Sacre et couronnement de Louis XVI* (detail), Paris, 1775.

Honorary and Service Uniforms

The only uniforms to be seen at Versailles and in the royal residences were those worn by pages, guards and domestic servants, who all wore the royal livery.

THE ROYAL LIVERY

The royal livery was worn by the servants in the royal castles, by the wardrobe personnel, entertainers, messengers, floor-polishers, chimney sweeps, porters, seamen, inspectors and other servants; in many cases it was the equivalent of the uniform worn by the employees of different companies today.

Since the reign of Louis XIV, the full royal livery had consisted of a coat in blue cloth, with collar and facings in crimson velvet, a waistcoat in scarlet wool cloth with gold braid, and crimson breeches. The braid on the coat (white braid against a background of red needlecord) completed the colour scheme that has since been associated with the French – blue, white and red.[12] Blue was introduced during the first two royal dynasties; red, during the third, lasting until Charles VI; and white was adopted from the reign of Charles VII. The breadth of the braid distinguished the full livery from humbler versions, while the ribbons worn on the shoulder and the position of the pockets – lengthwise or crosswise – distinguished the various services from one another.

THE PAGES

The royal livery was worn by the pages of the royal stables,[13] but eighteen of these, selected by the chief equerry, were allowed to wear gold braid as well. The pages of the bedchamber wore crimson velvet coats, braided all over; during the reign of Louis XVI these cost 1,500 *livres* each. Their hats were trimmed with a plume and a broad band in *point d'Espagne*. They also had a less extravagant outfit of scarlet wool, with silver and gold braid. The queen's twelve pages were dressed in red with gold braid. The comte d'Hézècques, who was a page at court a few years before the Revolution, recalled in his memoirs the pages of the comte de Provence, who were dressed in red with blue facings; the pages of the comte d'Artois had coats trimmed with amaranth; those of the duc d'Orléans wore red with gold frogging; finally, those of the prince de Condé wore daffodil yellow with red facings. The duty of all these children and young men was to accompany the king and the royal princes in order to light their way on the staircases, carry their trains and ride on the running board beside their carriages.

THE GUARDS

The king's bodyguards, numbering 1,300, were dressed in blue coats with red waistcoats, breeches and stockings, all trimmed with silver braid. Officers wore silver embroidery where the men wore braid, and did not wear red stockings; they carried a small ebony cane with an ivory knob. The guards who spent their day at the main gate to the royal residence wore the same uniform, but their braid was half silver, half gold. The so-called guardians of the king's sleeve, who had to stay at the king's elbow permanently, wore a *hoqueton*, a tunic thickly covered in gold and silver embroidery, over their uniform. On ceremonial occasions, the Swiss Guard still wore the traditional costume of the liberators of Switzerland: doublet and slashed hose, starched ruff, plumed hat. For everyday wear they had a blue coat *à la française* with gold braid, the rest of their clothing was red and they carried the traditional halberd. The military guards of the royal residence, who formed a kind of police corps, wore a pink, blue and white *hoqueton* and carried a club.

Court Dress

The perfect courtier had first to prove his degrees of lineage, and then to submit to the ritual of presentation at court.

For men, the ceremony of 'admission to the privileges of the court' took three days and required at least two outfits: a very elegant one for his presentation to the king on the first day and to the royal family on the third, and another to wear for the royal hunt on the second day. The second outfit consisted of a grey coat with a red waistcoat and breeches, riding boots, a small *chapeau français* (a three-cornered hat) with gold braid, and a hunting knife worn on one side.[14] Monsieur de Villeneuve Bargenon spent 348 *livres* on his hunting clothes in 1788, and this did not include his travel and living expenses.[15] The hunt had its own irritations, too, because the grooms took malicious pleasure in supplying newcomers with the most difficult mounts in the stable. Once these tests were passed, however, the newly presented courtiers could appear at receptions in half-gala dress (embroidered around the edges only) or, if circumstances so required, in full gala dress, in rich gold or silver fabric, embroidered all over. The waistcoat was of different fabric, as were the accessories on the coat.

For women, presentation at court was their chance to wear full court dress for the first time, an innovation during the reign of Louis XIV, modified in the eighteenth century, in outline at least, by the addition of paniers. The women's outfit comprised three separate parts: a closed, very rigid, whaleboned bodice, with a wide, oval neckline and half-sleeves consisting of layers of lace; a skirt, spread over immense paniers, often with a circumference of more than three ells (3m 60cm); a train, known as a *bas de robe*, which was hooked to the waist at the back and whose length was proportionate to the rank of its wearer. Madame d'Oberkirch's full court dress in 1784 was in 'gold brocade, with natural flowers. It contained not less than twenty-three ells of fabric and was enormously heavy.'

Women had to go into training for a few days to be able to bear the pain of the whaleboned bodice, which cut into the upper arms;

39. Engraving by J.-E. Nilson, *La Danse ordinaire*, *c.*1740. Full court dress.

they had to have lessons in curtsying from a dancing master in order to learn how to give the little kick required to get the yards of fabric into place when, after curtsying low several times, they had to retreat backwards from the royal presence without getting tangled up in their train.[16] Generally everything went well. One presentation at court, however, which was not as solemn as might have been hoped, was the presentation of the 'Lady Eon' on Sunday 2 November 1777. 'Her Ladyship' had just been notified of the order to wear the clothes appropriate to 'her' gender, that is, female clothing. In full court dress, with trimmings by Rose Bertin, fan in hand and diamonds at her neck and ears, suddenly, during mass in the Chapel at Versailles, she 'dropped her wig and headdress', which exposed 'her' perfectly ridiculous position. Some kindly bystander adjusted the gentleman's wig, and he reappeared in the chapel as if nothing had happened, carrying the train of his dress over his arm. He went straight up to the altar, fanning himself coquettishly with unruffled calm, and this made it all the more difficult for others there to keep a straight face. Madame Campion added: 'The long train of his dress and his layered sleeves contrasted strangely with his grenadier's gait and speech.'[17]

The presentation outfit was usually black. Madame de la Tour du Pin, however, contrary to the usual practice, was all in white because she was in the later stages of a period of mourning. Her white gown was adorned by some handsome jet beads and some diamonds lent to her by the queen; her skirt was embroidered all over with pearls and silver. The custom was to ransack all the family jewel caskets for the occasion and, if no jewellery was available, to borrow from someone; a loan from the queen was a mark of particular favour. Black lace lappets hung from the headdress. The following day the pervading black was exchanged for gold and coloured clothing. Thus attired, as called for by étiquette, a woman could attend mass, be present at the removal of the king's boots, at Christmas and New Year parties, and at Easter and Whitsun celebrations; she could attend full-dress balls, processions of the Order of the Holy Spirit, and the baptisms and marriages of members of the royal family – just as the men who were admitted to court privileges could do. The honour of participating in these select moments in the life of the sovereign compensated generously for the boredom of spending several hours getting dressed and of riding, fully clothed and coiffed, in a carriage from Paris to Versailles 'perpetually in fear of creasing ones skirt and furbelows'.[18]

'The ladies in waiting to the queen and Madame la Dauphine', Madame de Genlis wrote in her *Dictionnaire des étiquettes*, 'also wore full court dress, but without a train. Nor were they permitted to wear the whaleboned bodice, covered with fabric and often jewels as well, which young people wore. They had to make do with a *mantelet*.'

A few years before the French Revolution, when the wind of freedom was beginning to be felt, full court dress, which was heavy and uncomfortable, began to be worn only in exceptional circumstances. The grand *robe à la française*, which had almost the same line without the extreme rigidity of its predecessor, began to be preferred; its traditional circular pleat (now in use for nearly fifty years) gave it a certain dignity. This dress was permitted for court mourning in 1781, and in 1783 was recommended for ceremonial visits; women who had not had the foresight to put it on had to request special permission to be received by the queen or the princesses.[19]

In 1787, going one step further, a *robe ordinaire de cour* began to be tolerated. It was similar to the *robe à l'anglaise* and was worn over a simple pad at the back, a precursor of the bustle. Only the extravagance of the trimmings made it a ceremonial garment.

40. Engraving by Vossnik, after Leclerc, *Galerie des Modes et Costumes français* (reprinted by P. Cornu, plate 167). *Robe à la sultane* for a costume ball, 1782.

Costume Balls

Of all the entertainments held at court, the costume balls were amongst the most brilliant. The ladies singled out for dancing sat in the front row. They had to be in full court dress (which did not make fluid, graceful movement very easy, but somehow they managed miraculously) and to wear their hair curled. Their partners also had to have long hair, either lengthened with hair pieces or with a wig that ended in a single curl. It was not the dance itself that was individually prized, but the sight of the whole room: 'when the royal family make their entrance, when the whole court is gathered together . . . it is magnificent because of the quantity and brilliance of the jewellery, the gold and silver embroidery, the wonderful fabrics. Unless you have seen it you can have no idea what it is like,' exclaimed Madame d'Oberkirch with characteristic enthusiasm. At the costume ball thrown in honour of the comte and comtesse du Nord all the courtiers were dressed in their best finery, and the women who were to dance wore dominoes in white satin with small paniers and small trains. 'The party does not go on very late', Madame d'Oberkirch added, 'these formal gatherings are not amusing. Once you have seen the crowd you start wanting to leave.' She remembered a small, impromptu ball held after dinner at the residence of the princesse de Lamballe with much more pleasure: 'It was incomparably much more fun than the other.'

The balls given by Queen Marie-Antoinette were a little more relaxed. The costumes were elegant but simple. The men wore dress suits and danced with their plumed hat on their head, 'an extremely noble and graceful practice', declared the comte d'Hézècques, who had witnessed such a practice only at the French court: 'Some of the men wear black coats embroidered with jet and the light glinting off the embroidery makes a particularly brilliant impression.' Once the king had left, etiquette relaxed somewhat.

The older 'young people', too old to want to take part in the official entertainment, danced the quadrille or an English line dance. They could be recognised by their bare heads, because they were supposed 'not to have come to dance, and therefore had not dressed up'.[20]

Clothes for the Royal Châteaux

Customs and manners changed somewhat when the court was on the move. Special clothes were worn in each of the *châteaux* visited. For

41. Engraving by Dupin, after Leclerc, *Galerie des Modes et Costumes français* (reprinted by P. Cornu, plate 77). Formal dress at Choisy, 1779.

men it was red embroidered with gold for the Trianon, green for Compiègne, blue for Choisy. At Rambouillet hunting parties were held and only hunters were invited: the outfit worn here was made of thick, blue cloth with gold braid. The arrangement of the braid indicated which animal was being hunted: green was the colour worn for hunting with a shotgun. All those accompanying the king were dressed like him. When women were invited they were sometimes allowed to wear different clothes, which is how the grand *robe à la française* made its first appearance at court.

The King's Patent Jerkin

A few items of clothing were worn only by the privileged, and meant that they were admitted to places closed to others. This was the case with the 'patent' jerkin, officially established by two decrees, on 29 December 1664 and 16 January 1665, but which actually goes back to a decision taken by Louis XIV at the end of 1661. The sovereign intended thereby to distinguish the small band of courtiers who were permanently authorised to follow him when hunting or out walking. 'In blue silk or moiré, trimmed with braid and frogging, lace or embroidery in gold or silver in form and manner', presented by His Majesty, lined with red, with a red waistcoat: it constituted a real uniform, although its cut followed fashion as it developed, and it also exempted its wearer from the sumptuary laws which at the time regulated the wearing of gold and silver. Permission to wear the jerkin was accompanied by a patent or licence signed by the king, and certainly in the case of Louis XIV was never granted to more than fifty people at a time.[21] Under the Regency the number grew, then decreased to eighteen between 1723 and 1750, when the wearing of gold and silver ceased to be controlled by law. After that the 'patent' jerkin seems to have fallen into disuse.

The Uniform of Bellevue

Madame de Pompadour created a uniform for her château at Bellevue and designed its embroidery herself. It was a regulation outfit for men made of fine purple cloth, with a broad band of gold embroidery around the edge and the buttonholes; it was worn with a waistcoat in plain pale grey satin, without any gold. Worn only by those who were permitted to accompany the marquise at her château, it revived Louis XIV's original idea for the 'patent' jerkin.

The Legal Profession

The gradual adoption of short clothes by men during the Middle Ages was ignored by certain state officials with formal positions of responsibility, who preferred to retain their long robes as their professional attire. In this way, members of the State Council, the Audit Office, and the Parlement, plus all the lawyers and notaries in the courts, municipal magistrates, members of universities and the clergy, found themselves, in the eighteenth century, wearing costumes that were a direct legacy of medieval dress; only accessories such as gloves and wigs (the latter already a little out of date) reflected contemporary fashion. The fabrics and colours differed according to the profession and where it was exercised, but the basic shape of the garments remained more or less the same everywhere. The outfit generally consisted of a cassock, belted at the waist, and a very full cloak, also known as a 'robe', open down the front.

At the coronation, the state counsellors wore a black cloak with a train and wide sleeves over a black satin cassock, belted with a black watered silk sash with gold tassels. Members of the Audit Office also wore a black cassock: presidents wore velvet, *maîtres* wore damask, examiners wore satin and auditors wore taffeta.

The chancellor and officials of the Parlement, to whom the king's authority was delegated, were robed in red, the colour of sovereignty: the senior magistrates wore a round flat cap made of velvet, trimmed with gold braid, royal headgear that can be seen on the head of St Louis in one of the stained glass windows in the Sainte-Chapelle. The chancellor, clad all in red, wore a cassock of satin with a girdle of silk, a long cloak open down the right side, lined and edged with ermine, with a matching *pèlerine* and a flat-topped *mortier* or cap made of cloth of gold. The senior president of the Parlement was similarly dressed but had only two rows of gold braid on his cap, whilst the presidents '*à mortier*' (with cap) had only one. Magistrates not qualified to wear a mortar wore a red stuffed band on their shoulder, the last vestige of the hood worn by them until 1500. The red costume was worn only for special functions: for normal audiences, black clothing similar to

42. Carle Van Loo, *Michel-Etienne Turgot, Merchants' Leader*, *c*.1730. Musée des Arts Décoratifs, Paris.

that worn by members of provosts', bailiffs' and seneschals' courts was worn. When present at the *Parlement* on solemn occasions, barristers also wore red robes, while solicitors wore black.

The costume worn by municipal magistrates differed from town to town. In Paris[22] the *prévôt des marchands* (the merchants' leader, chief municipal magistrate and president of the municipal council) and the four aldermen who assisted him, plus the clerk of the court and the officer, all wore a robe that was red on the right side (the magisterial colour) and tan (the livery of nearly all merchants) on the left; the tan worn by the *prévôt* was lighter in shade than the others, and he wore it with a red cassock; all the other cassocks were black. The members of the city council and the officials responsible for each *quartier* of Paris wore black silk robes. The prosecutor, the king's representative, was entirely dressed in red. The ushers were the only officials still wearing the red and blue two-coloured robes that had been worn by municipal officials until about 1500.

In Toulouse[23] the *capitouls* or local magistrates wore a long robe covered by an *aumusse* or almuce, a kind of full chasuble lined with white, with a large epaulette on either side in red embroidered with gold, and three rows of white fur that hung over the top of the sleeve. This was often replaced by the *habit à la française*. In this case only the *aumusse* was worn, red on the right, black on the left, with a long red stole fixed on to the left shoulder, contrasting sharply with the black. The black biretta was also replaced by a hat.

In Bordeaux[24] in the eighteenth century the *jurats*, as the municipal magistrates were known, wore a wide-sleeved robe over their ordinary clothing. This was white velvet on the right side and red silk on the other. For the grand entry of the governors this was replaced by a red and white satin robe, lined with red taffeta. On their heads barristers wore a *toque* with a very small brim, nobles wore a big black plumed hat and the *jurats* a circular flat-topped cap.

University costume[25] after the sixteenth century varied according to town and faculty. In Paris the faculty of theology was still wearing the ancient, full cope in black silk, completely closed, with slits for the arms, and with a short *camail* or hood over the shoulders. The faculty of medicine wore a black *simarre* (cassock) with a front-opening scarlet cope and a full hood. In the faculty of arts the gown, red after 1721, was worn with a hood of *menu vair* (miniver), a kind of blue-grey squirrel fur. The faculty of law wore a red gown with wide sleeves and black silk lapels; this was worn over a black cassock with a black sash. The scarlet hood was worn over the left shoulder and was edged with ermine. Bands began to be worn in the seventeenth century. All these costumes were for lectures and public ceremonies rather than for everyday wear: when doctors visited their patients, they, of course, wore ordinary street clothes.

The secular clergy dressed like lawyers until 1500; in the eighteenth century they wore a long *soutane* or cassock to go to church, celebrate mass and for the exercise of their religious duties outside. The *soutane* was so named because for centuries it was an undergarment, worn covered by a gown. By the middle of the eighteenth century it had acquired the dignity of clerical costume and was worn on top, and had been adopted in nearly every diocese in France. However, the *soutanelle*, a shorter version that priests wore when travelling was sometimes replaced by a jerkin or redingote. Abbots received at court were considered to be travelling and therefore wore the *habit à la française*, with a short straight cape in pleated black taffeta, shoes with large buckles, a wig with two ringlets and black breeches; the insignia of their calling were the bands which, around 1750, changed from white to black with a white border.[26]

Perhaps, as religious costume is being discussed, the clothing worn by canonesses should be mentioned here. Canonesses were noblewomen who had taken no vows and who did not live in religious communities but in private houses. They served on a rota basis at palaces such as Versailles, and could re-enter the world or get married provided they renounced their benefice. They were also permitted to select a 'niece' to succeed them: in other words, they had the best of all worlds, enjoying the freedom of married women 'without a husband to annoy them', as the baronne d'Oberkirch put it when talking about the canonesses of the Abbaye de Remiremont.

The canonesses did not wear ceremonial dress at court; the black silk dress, with fashionable bonnet and church cloak in black light silk, generously bordered with ermine, and with a long train that had to be carried by pages, was worn only for mass and vespers in the abbey. At home and in society they wore coloured dresses and cloaks. Madame de Genlis, who was received into the church at Aix when she was seven, the age at which a vote for the election of a new abbess could be cast, remembers that 'the celebrant put a consecrated gold ring on her finger, and attached to her head a small piece of black and white cloth, the length of a finger, which the canonesses called a husband (*mari*)', and 'handed her the insignia of the order: a red cord and an enamelled cross, and a broad belt made of moiré'. Madame d'Oberkirch describes the cross of the canonesses of Remiremont, which bore a picture of Saint Romain, founder of the order, and which was worn 'attached to a broad blue ribbon with a red border, worn from right to left like a sash'.

The Uniforms of the States General

In accordance with the custom of the court, ceremonial costume had to be worn by the deputies convened to the *Etats Généraux*, or States General. The *Moniteur Universel* of 6–14 May 1789 carries a description of the various uniforms. In the case of the clergy, cardinals had to be dressed in a red cope; archbishops and bishops in a *rochet, camail* or short cape, purple cassock and square biretta; abbots, deans, canons, parish priests and others in a cassock, long cloak and square biretta. Deputies who belonged to the nobility wore a coat and cloak made of fabric to suit the time of year; the cloak was trimmed with gold fabric and the waistcoat was made of the same gold stuff. They also wore black breeches, white stockings, a lace cravat and a hat with white feathers curled back in the fashion made popular by Henri IV, like the hat worn by knights of the Order of the Holy Spirit.

Deputies belonging to the Third Estate wore a coat, waistcoat and breeches of black wool with black stockings and a short silk or voile cloak 'like the one generally worn at court by the legal profession', a muslin cravat, a hat with the brim turned back on three sides, without braid or buttons, 'like the hat worn by ecclesiastics when wearing a short coat'. Lack of historical references – the last convening of the States General had been during the reign of Louis XIII – meant that the style of the costume had to be borrowed from that of the Church or the legal profession, or of officials taking part in the king's coronation.

These costumes were not particularly welcomed, particularly by the Third Estate, and they were promptly argued against by the Constituent Assembly and renounced on Thursday, 15 October 1789, primarily because they emphasised the distinction between the three orders of society which the Assembly hoped to abolish; but also because they had been imposed. The idea was that, from now on, uniforms would be created by the Assembly for itself, although the necessity for wearing uniforms as external markers for state employees, to indicate the functions they performed and the authority vested in them, was recognised.

Thus the idea of costume as a series of semi-religious vestments worn for the worship of the royal personage, or as a sign of belonging to his service, gave way to the idea of costume as a sign of delegation power, and this was the origin of the great proliferation of civil uniforms in the nineteenth century.

Chapter Eight

The World of Elegance

Whether the king at any given period was interested in dress or not, he occupied the highest point in the social hierarchy and had to dress to suit his position and rank: his costume was taken charge of by his wardrobe, which was well equipped to deal with any eventuality. The wardrobe constituted an administrative department of its own. It was directed by a grand master, assisted by two under masters, and had a large team of staff: a treasurer, a keeper of the clothes, tailoring boys, valets, wardrobe boys, washerwomen for body linen, women to look after the lace, casket minders, baggage carriers, mule drivers, and such like. Orders would be placed regularly with a wide range of suppliers. It was the custom to have a dozen coats made for the sovereign each season – coats to be worn in the morning, coats for reviewing the troops, for hunting, for public levées and, of course, for Sundays and ceremonies. These were extravagantly gorgeous garments, to be worn with the famous royal diamonds – the Regent in the hat and the Sancy on the epaulette that held the *cordon bleu*. Over and above the twelve basic outfits were clothes for mourning, birth, baptisms and royal weddings, plus clothes for visits by foreign monarchs. Informal dress was not included and was not renewed every year.

Louis xv knew how to get the best out of his wardrobe staff. When he realised that the coat presented to him for the marriage of the duc de Chartres was the most beautiful garment he had ever seen, he requested that it be kept for the marriage of his grandson, the future Louis xvi. Conversely, when at the beginning of his reign the young King Louis xvi had to give orders to the grand master of the wardrobe for the first time, he requested only six coats of grey ratteen;[1] fortunately, the wardrobe staff took him in hand and dressed him like a king. Thanks to them the royal wardrobe contained not only coats and frock coats in grey frieze or brown wool, but also costumes in apricot-coloured wool with grey spots, in cerise velvet with black spots, in lilac moiré with a white glaze, plain or enhanced with silk embroidery or with spangles, sequins, *cannetillé* or silver, mixed with coloured semi-precious stones; dressing gowns made of satin for winter wear, or, for warmer weather, made of *gros de Naples* or *poult-de-soie*, embroidered in silk or silk and gold.[2] The comte d'Hézècques convincingly suggests that, dressed in his finery and standing still (his gait was a little awkward), Louis XVI cut a noble figure. An unfortunate adventure befell him, however, one day: the queen had to recall him from a hunt to tell him of the unexpected arrival of the Count of Haga, who was none other than the King of Sweden. Owing to the time of day, the king's wardrobe staff were not at Versailles and the keys to the cupboards could not be found; the king was dressed by courtiers in whatever clothes they could lay their hands on. He eventually appeared in a red velvet waistcoat (in June), one gold and one silver shoe buckle and his sashes and badges all awry. He was powdered on one side only and his sword knot kept slipping. The queen was not amused. The king himself laughed it off and made the Count of Haga laugh too – the latter was able to comment favourably on his royal host's benevolence and serenity. This, at any rate, is how Madame d'Oberkirch described the incident, and one may assume that she was well informed.

The people surrounding the sovereign must have spent a lot of money maintaining their position in society. In 1745 the duc de Chartres and the duc de Penthièvre attended the wedding of the Dauphin, son of Louis XV, wearing coats with buttonholes edged with diamonds, embroidered in gold and trimmed with *point d'Espagne*. The marquis de Stainville wore a coat of cloth of silver embroidered with gold and lined with sable. Each of these outfits cost a great deal. Contemporary chroniclers mention the sum of 15,000 *livres*, which is probably no exaggeration, bearing in mind that some fabrics cost as much as 150 or 160 *livres* an ell, that it takes nine ells to make a coat and to that must be added the cost of embroidery with semi-precious stones or precious metals. For the same ceremony the marquis de Mirepoix rented three outfits at a cost of 6,000 *livres*, and returned them to the tailor afterwards.[3] Obtaining appropriate clothes could push courtiers into debt, and sometimes to quite a considerable degree; when Louis XVI complimented M. de C. . . on the elegance of his garb, all those at court laughed heartily because they were well aware of the financial straits the poor man was in when he replied, 'Sire, I owe it to you.'[4]

When not attending formal functions, courtiers were satisfied with dressing like other men and women of fashion. It was no longer only the court that dictated what was fashionable; after the Regency, Paris began to set the tone as much as the court. When the town got too carried away by innovations, however, the court was there to maintain a certain respect for propriety and tradition.

Paris fashions could be a bit showy at times. From the reign of Louis XV onwards the sumptuary laws ceased to be respected. Not a great deal of attention had been paid to them, in fact, at any time, but at least they were regularly renewed. This was no longer the case in the eighteenth century. People dressed according to their means rather than according to their condition.[5] Even members of the classes that hitherto had had a reputation for sobriety and careful management of their wealth sometimes gave way to temptation, spending their money on frivolous and costly fashions. Monsieur de Caumartin, a *conseiller d'Etat* or senior government functionary, who died in 1720, was the first member of the legal profession to wear velvet. A little later a lesser legal luminary dressed in the fashion of what came to be known as the 'dandy' in the nineteenth century: he wore 'a billowing wig, bands tied like a cravat, stockings with zig-zags and his robe hitched up to the fourth button; a lackey carried his train'.[6] As the Revolution approached, other such fops used to dine in a tailcoat and round hat and called it 'English simplicity'. Quite a few gentlemen ceased to wear a sword except when formally dressed. Members of the lower classes followed, and no authority on earth would have had the strength to stem the tide of fashion. Thus a tradition of the French nobility that was centuries old was summarily abandoned.

At Versailles, however, with the exception of the comte d'Artois and his friends, who welcomed the innovations launched by the Paris fops, men were on the whole loyal to tradition. Madame de la Tour du Pin remembers seeing her fiancé, Monsieur de Gouvernet, wearing an elegant black or dark steel-grey tailcoat one morning during a period of deep mourning at court. She saw him again at dinner time (today's lunch time) in formal dress with a sword: 'a well-bred gentleman would never have wanted to be seen at Versailles dressed in any other fashion'.

Like the king, the queen also had a full retinue of wardrobe staff: a master, three valets, a tailor, a collar-maker, an embroidress, a woman to starch the sleeves worn at court, three hairdressers and a secretary,

43. Jean-Marc Nattier, *Queen Marie Leczinska*, 1742. Musée du Château, Versailles.

all under the direction of a lady-in-waiting, who placed the orders and paid the bills.

The pious, modest Marie Leczinska regarded the formalities as her inevitable lot and allowed herself to be dressed as a queen when necessary, changing her clothes at least three times a day. She was happiest, nevertheless, as Nattier painted her in his celebrated portrait, wearing a simple *robe à la française*, with a black lace mantilla over her small peaked cap. The artist has captured her engrossed in her favourite pastime, reading. A woman of inexhaustible good will, she would listen to concerts from her room at Fontainebleau so that the court ladies would not have to undergo the agony of wearing the full whaleboned bodices that would have been obligatory had she been present at the concert itself. Nor were her daughters interested in being leaders of fashion. As the years passed they complied more and more mechanically with court ceremonial; for example, when called to attend the ceremony of removing the king's boots after the hunt, they would simply put a great panier with a skirt trimmed with gold or embroidery over their normal clothes, tie a long train round their waist and cover the informality of the upper part of their clothing with a short black taffeta cape that came right up to the chin, covering everything.[7]

The mirror of fashion at this period was Louis XV's mistress, Madame de Pompadour. She had no hesitation in dressing up in 'painted' (that is, printed) fabrics when these were absolutely prohibited. She gave printed cottons to her friends as presents and protected some of the clandestine workshops where they were made, encouraging consumers to defy the government's ruling and hastening the repeal of the law. It was she who introduced the oriental influence into French wardrobes through some of the theatrical roles she played, and it was she who improvised the 'Mahon' style of tying a necktie for the duc de Richelieu, after the capture of Menorca. It was also Madame de Pompadour who revived the custom first established by Louis XIV, and herself designed the Bellevue uniform for close personal friends whom she invited to visit her at her château.

Madame du Barry succeeded Madame de Pompadour in the king's affections, but was not someone who influenced fashion. She was indifferent to clothes, preferring a certain romantic carelessness in dress, soft, loosely knotted hair, and the simple little gowns that she wore to dine with the king. And, although she encouraged the luxury trade by buying informal gowns in *point d'Angleterre* at 4,000 *livres* each, and by making gifts of clothing to the king, to the duc de Richelieu and even to Lekain (she gave him a theatrical costume), she did not possess the taste to be a leader of fashion. As a very young girl she had been employed by the fashion store Labille, performing duties there that must have been similar to those performed by the models of today.

By contrast, as soon as Marie-Antoinette became queen, she was keen to exercise her royal prerogative to the full. To the dismay of the champions of conventional behaviour, she received her suppliers in her private chambers, since she was not allowed to admit them to the royal apartments. Every morning when she awoke, while she was still in her nightwear, she chose her clothes for the day by marking little samples of her dresses with pins; the dresses arrived shortly afterwards in large baskets lined with green taffeta. Her choice of clothes reflected her own taste, not that of her lady-in-waiting.[8]

Marie-Antoinette was young and good looking, with the bearing of a queen, and was always eager to be up to date. She became the focus of interest for fashionable society (everyone wanted to be dressed like Her Majesty) and the prey of the fashion trade – wig-makers, for example, who saw her as the ideal person to popularise their ideas and designs. Thus began a period when fantasy reigned supreme, some of it contentious and all of it expensive. Contentious hair-styles included the 'elevated' one embellished with muslin sails, which were hoisted one day in 1779 by two hundred ladies who had

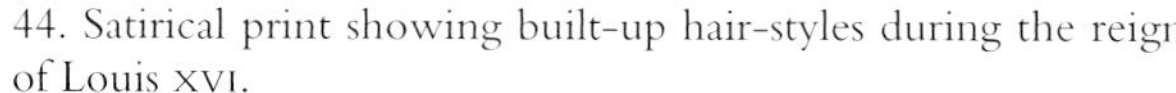

44. Satirical print showing built-up hair-styles during the reign of Louis XVI.

come to Versailles to congratulate the queen on having recently given birth. The duc de Croÿ thought for a moment that he was in the presence of the whole French fleet.[9] Mademoiselle Bertin, who ran the most popular of the fashion stores, and whose bi-weekly conversations with the queen earned her the nickname of 'Minister of Fashion', was so intoxicated by her own success that she used sometimes to send bills (which were frequently not itemised) for sums of the order of 6,000 *livres* or more for a single outfit. Louis XVI was not at all happy with the extravagances forced upon him by his wife, and, having observed the top row of plumes on her headdress being removed to enable her to get into her carriage, presented her with a more modest diamond aigrette which he hoped would suffice for her as headgear. However, the policy of Monsieur de Calonne, the minister of finance, was to spend a lot in order to appear rich; he would not have dreamed of complaining as the bills piled up. At this rate, of course, the 120,000 *livres* allotted to pay for the twelve major court outfits, the twelve charming little gowns and the twelve dresses for intimate suppers and games in the small apartments, ordered three times a year by the queen, were never sufficient;[10] it took the royal exchequer several years to settle accounts.

In spite of the efforts of the comtesse d'Ossun, appointed lady-in-waiting in 1781, to try to set the account books in order, and in spite of the queen's earnest resolutions – bereavements, worries over the 'Affair of the Necklace' and the approach of her thirtieth birthday (then the threshold of old age) had caused her to give up 'feathers, flowers and the colour pink', in other words to give up the frivolous ways of a young woman accustomed to adulation – expenditure continued to rise.

In defence of Marie-Antoinette, it must be said that the balance between simplicity and the required level of dignity was not always easy to achieve. Except when engaged in ceremonial duties, she liked to be dressed comfortably, and in the summer, at Trianon or on the terrace at Versailles, in the company of the comtesse de Provence, the comtesse d'Artois and a few friends, she would wear a *gaulle* or a *chemise à la reine*. The style was first borrowed from creole women by the ladies of Bordeaux and was the forerunner of the muslin gowns worn during the Consulate, the Directoire and the Empire. But this clothing was not deemed suitable for a queen of France, and when Madame Vigée-Lebrun exhibited her portrait of the queen dressed in this fashion at the Salon of 1783, the painting had to be withdrawn because visitors to the exhibition disapproved of it so much. As often happens when a public figure is not well liked, she was blamed for everything, whether justly or unjustly; it is undeniable, however, that Marie-Antoinette's extravagance in matters of dress, especially in her youth, weighed heavily against her when the Revolution came.

In matters of fashion, nevertheless, her influence was a positive one. She had a feeling for future trends, demonstrated not only in her taste for muslin gowns but also in her romantic historical sense: at costume balls she showed a strong penchant for the period of Gabrielle d'Estrées (puffed sleeves, black hat with white feathers). Whether consciously or not, she made women's clothing (as was remarked by a contemporary chronicler) 'a political matter, through her influence on commerce and manufacture'.

Every society lady wanted to imitate her. Fashionable women of the period spent half their day paying or receiving calls, dining in town, going to the theatre, balls or the opera, or simply walking up and down the single alley in the Jardin des Tuileries where it was smart to be seen. The rest of their time was devoted to getting dressed in the succession of different outfits necessary for the pursuit of this social whirl. In the morning it was enough to put one's hair in order and the first calls would be made in informal dress. Later, a second toilette would be required to construct a more elaborate hair-style. Before important visits or big social events the assistance of a wig-maker and a dressmaker would be required. Even kept women were very carefully turned out and could not be distinguished from their respectable sisters – for whom they hoped to be mistaken.

During the course of the day clothes and fashion must have been the subject of a good many conversations; the language used was probably quite clear to women at the time, but now seems hopelessly enigmatic, like a coded message, the key to which has been lost.

Today very little remains of the glamorous clothes worn at court and about town. The sale of the queen's dresses (and the king's coats), were welcome perks for the lady-in-waiting and the grand master of the wardrobe. Royal clothing, once sold, always had to be remade because none of it could reappear at Versailles in its original state. Unless it had been acquired simply as a souvenir (but nobody could have foreseen the tragic fate of Louis XVI and Marie-Antoinette), the wardrobes of the king and queen must have provided the raw materials for a number of church vestments, soft furnishings or re-cut and re-made garments.[11] Members of high society, through their valets and chambermaids, supplied the second-hand clothing shops where discarded clothes could be bought. A few families, however, kept all or part of the wardrobe of a particular ancestor, like the dress that belonged to the marquise de Blangy, appointed 'lady to accompany' Princess Elisabeth in 1784. Although this dress was transformed into an ecclesiastical cope during the nineteenth century, the whole front of the skirt was retrievable. The pieces were restored to their original position and were exhibited at the Musée du Costume in Paris and manage to convey something of the elegance that must have pertained to Versailles during the last days of the Ancien Régime.

Chapter Nine

Clothes for the Working Class

Any overview of French dress in the eighteenth century would be incomplete without mention of working-class clothing, which was worn by vast numbers of people. Domestic servants, small tradespeople, artisans, labourers, peasants – the way each category dressed differed according to their place of residence – Paris or the provinces, town or country – to the frequency of contact they enjoyed with high society, to the nature of their employment and to the extent to which local tradition had survived in the area.

There were Parisians who came into daily contact with clients of the great tailors and who thus spent their lives consumed by envy of high fashion. 'Monsieur Nicolas', wrote Restif de la Bretonne, 'having spent the day at the printworks wearing labourer's clothes, put on a well-fitting coat of ratteen, breeches of black drugget and white cotton stockings, took his handsome opera hat with the silk braid border under his arm, attached a small sword with a steel hilt to his belt and, with hair curled and pomaded, walking on tip-toe in order not to dirty his patent leather shoes with their copper buckles, set off through the muddy streets, where he was taken for a knight or a marquis. . . . The most modest *grisette*, the poorest working woman owns elegant (if inexpensive) outfits for wearing on high days and holidays, and is anxious that her feet should look small, wearing narrow shoes in brilliantly coloured leather with very high heels and rosettes of ribbon'.[1] Already in 1730 servants were beginning to adopt the panier, the latest fashion craze, and in 1756 the marquis de Mirabeau complained of paying profuse compliments to a man wearing a coat of black silk drugget and a well-powdered wig who turned out to be 'his saddler's head assistant.'[2] The sumptuary laws had disappeared and class dictated no fashion regulations.

People in the provinces were a little behind the latest fads in Paris; they had contact with the aristocracy, however, in the shape of minor nobles who sometimes left their town houses or châteaux to go to Versailles and would return with news of the new fashions. The gap

45. Engraving by Le Beau, after Leclerc, *Galerie des Modes et Costumes français* (reprinted by P. Cornu, plate 11). Cook, newly arrived in Paris, 1778.

that had formed between Paris and the provinces during the Regency gradually disappeared. The provinces were a major source of domestic servants for people living in Paris, and newly arrived staff quickly learned to dress coquettishly, like the cook (fig. 45), engraved for the *Galerie des Modes et Costumes français*, who 'began to assume the elegant airs of a Parisian', with her smartly trimmed *fichu*. For such people, clothes were no longer an accurate indicator of class or rank.

Finally, the peasantry constituted the main bulk of the population and showed no inclination to escape from their lowly status. Some continued to respect local traditions on feast days, but in general they dressed according to their means: 'traditional' regional costume did not really come into being until the nineteenth century. Nevertheless, travellers noticed that the countrywomen in Basse Provence wore red skirts and grey hats with floral or silver ribbons, whereas those in Haute Provence wore dresses of coarse brown wool, pleated on the hips; peasants in the Vallée du Campan were wrapped in fine brown wool cloaks and wore white hoods; the women of Normandy wore cambric headdresses, with points like wings attached to a cardboard sugarloaf. In Brittany the peasants wore rough cloth or *berlingue*, a mixture of hemp and wool. In the Albigeois men wore rough cloth or black or grey wool, whereas women preferred colour: yellow, red or blue skirts, petticoats and jerkins. In the Auvergne coarse wool in grey or brown was worn. Shoes were not worn everywhere: quite often clogs or *sabots* were worn instead.

This apparent diversity in fact concealed many common elements, particularly in men's clothing. The same coat, the same waistcoat and the same breeches were worn by all except for men of fashion; the shape of clothes developed along similar lines in the provinces, although things changed more slowly, as it took time for innovations to reach country districts. Fabrics were simpler: plain wools, linen or hemp sometimes locally produced, and there was a general absence of trimmings; these were the fabrics used for best clothes, at any rate – for Sundays and feast days. Working clothes consisted of a shirt and jerkin.

Women's basic attire had not changed for centuries and was highly functional; the same garments remained in use until the end of the nineteenth century, at least in the country and amongst the inhabitants of small towns. In the nineteenth century, women wore a shortish gathered skirt, a *casaquin* with a basque, the latter of varying length, and an apron with a bib pinned to the chest. The *casaquin* was often a shortened version of a *robe à la française*, split at the hips and with a back pleat that was visible from behind (though sometimes pulled in at the waist by the apron strings); the back-pleat earned the garment the name of *casaquin à la française*. If it was waisted it would be termed a *casaquin à l'anglaise* because of its similarity to the dress of that name.

These outfits were worn without paniers or whaleboned bodices by the housewives and servants painted going comfortably about their business by Chardin. The whaleboned bodice was in fact replaced by a corset which, unlike the modern garment of the same name, was a

46. Engraving by J. L. Delignon, after Moreau le Jeune, *The Landowner visiting his Tenant Farmer*, 1783.

soft undergarment made of thick cotton. One detail borrowed from the world of fashion was the cuffs, painted by Chardin *en raquette* (flat and flared) between 1733 and 1748, then flounced and finally *en sabot* (tight fitting and puffed around the elbow). The head was always covered: a lacy cap for town dwellers and a simple cloth headdress for peasant women; in the following century this headdress became the main feature of regional dress. A white fichu, plain or trimmed, covered the chest. To go outside women wrapped themselves in large capes with hoods, usually edged with a flat frill; these were part of rural costume for many years. For labouring in the fields peasants, men and women alike, wore shirts with capacious armholes; the chest was covered but the arms left free.

The similarity between working-class and fashionable dress can be explained partly by the spirit of imitation, but was due to a great extent to the practice of selling clothes to second-hand dealers or of giving them to domestic servants after they had been worn by their masters. With a little alteration they could begin a second career on the backs of their servants. Differences arose sometimes because of regional variations, but the difference was mainly due to the need to be comfortable when working.

High society took to a different kind of dress during the reign of Louis XVI, as has already been observed: simplicity became the order of the day. Men wore soft wool when they were not required to dress up; women borrowed their maidservants' *caracos* and skirts for wearing informally in the morning, although they would have them made up in slightly more luxurious fabrics. In the engraving by Moreau le Jeune entitled *The Landowner visiting his Tenant Farmer*, the farmer and his wife are dressed up to receive the visit in clothes that are almost more elegant than those worn by their master and his wife.

CHAPTER TEN

Fashion and Current Events

COURT DRESS WAS FOR CENTURIES INFLUENCED by current events, ever on the move and ever changing. The eighteenth century was crowded with events and discoveries of all kinds, culminating in the Revolution, when the structure of society was radically challenged. The tendency for current events to be reflected in costume became even more pronounced. As the century wore on the number of people interested in fashion increased, and a specialised press made its appearance, the latter improving communication in the field of dress enormously. Fashion as we understand it today – the deliberate quest for change for its own sake – came into being at this time and was nurtured to an extent by current events.

From 1778, when the *Galerie des Modes et Costumes français* was first published, to be followed in 1785 by the *Cabinet des Modes*, dressmakers' designs were bound together in collections and widely circulated. The speed with which innovations of every kind succeeded each other can be observed; their inspiration might be a naval battle or a popular song, a scientific discovery or a play, climaxing of course in the events of the Revolution. It may seem strange that politics should be reflected in a field apparently so frivolous as fashion, but the reason was precisely because political changes reflected current preoccupations, and although individuals were affected in different ways, these preoccupations were nevertheless very real. 'There is no doubt that a revolution like the one now taking place in France', according to the *Magasin des Modes* on 21 September 1789, 'is bound to provide some fashion ideas; it is an event of such importance.'

Before the Revolution one of the events that caught people's imagination sufficiently to be reflected in their dress was the Battle of Ouessant in 1779, when the French trounced the English at sea. Frenchwomen of fashion, with no apparent fear of ridicule, celebrated the victory by perching a miniature copy of the *Belle-Poule*, one of the ships engaged in the combat,[1] on top of their enormous wigs. Also in 1779 the capture of the island of Grenada by the comte

47. *Collection de la Parure des Dames*, no. 3, 1778. Hair-style *à la Belle-Poule*.

d'Estaing was responsible for the creation of the *chapeau à la Grenade*,[2] decorated with *grenades*, (pomegranates). A traditional song, *Marlborough s'en va-t-en-guerre*, revived by the nurses of the royal children and popular from then on, engendered dresses and trimmings *à la Marlborough*.[3] The first balloon flights by the Montgolfier brothers in 1783 and 1784 were the origin of hats *à la Montgolfier*, *à la Blanchard* (the inventor of the parachute), or *au demi-ballon*, and of the bonnet *au globe*.[4] Beaumarchais was the most successful author to influence fashion with his *Mariage de Figaro* and *Tarare*, the latter an opera libretto; between them the two works produced enormous numbers of jackets *à la Suzanne*, *caracos à la Chérubin*, costumes *au grand Figaro* and hats *à la Tarare*,[5] all of them garments or accessories often with very little to do with the characters whose names they bore, but which testified to the popular success of those characters.

The skirts of men's waistcoats offered the ideal surface for embroiderers to depict all sorts of little scenes, from busts of Voltaire and Rousseau in a landscape of poplars[6] (which gives an indication of the homage paid to the two philosophers, who both died in 1778) to the entire Assembly of Notables, summoned to an exceptional sitting in 1787 by an optimistic Calonne; the Montgolfiers' hot air balloons made their appearance too, of course.

After 1789 the coat *à la Révolution*, the frock *nationale* and the gown *à la Constitution* referred to the political upheavals taking place in France at the time – although, in spite of their names, they closely resembled other garments of the period. Silk trimmings 'with the three [social] orders united' bore an embroidered design based on the crozier, the shovel and the sword; shoe buckles *à la Bastille* were shaped like a plan of the prison; the motto 'to conquer or to die'[7] was embroidered on waistcoats – all these made direct reference to historical events. In 1790, when the Champ-de-Mars was being prepared for the Fête de la Fédération (to celebrate the first anniversary of the storming of the Bastille in 1789), men working on the site wore special clothes for the occasion: a pair of drill breeches with well-pulled up white silk stockings below, and beautifully polished shoes with rosettes',[8] clothing that was designed to look like theatrical clothing to celebrate a very dramatic occasion.

Finally, there was one category of accessories which by definition made reference to current events: these were the revolutionary fans. Their frame was made of fruit wood or mahogany, and the pleated paper bore a coloured print on one side and a song on the other. These were also commentaries on some, but not all important events. The most popular themes were the birth of the duke of Normandy (the future Louis XVII), the Assembly of Notables, the meeting of the States General, the storming of the Bastille, Parisians at Versailles, the confiscation of clergy property, the *Fête de la Fédération* and the Declaration of the Rights of Man.

Chapter Eleven

Dress, Politics and Ideology during the Revolution

Dress is so intimately linked to life that it could not fail to be affected by the Revolution, the great upheaval that caused France's transformation from a monarchy by divine right to a sovereign nation. The taste for symbols remained or even increased, but the meaning of the symbols changed.

In addition to the simple fashion accessories, discussed in the previous chapter, that mirrored political events, each citizen could now express his political convictions in the way he dressed: colour symbolism played a very important role in the process. For those who wholly supported the new ideas, the three colours combined (white to represent the king, plus the blue and red of the city of Paris) became the national emblem. The *tricolore* was adopted spontaneously in July 1789 to celebrate the reconciliation of Louis XVI with the people of Paris; subsequently a three-coloured cockade became the official mark that every French person was obliged to wear on his or her hat or in a buttonhole.[1] Thousands and thousands of them were sold and this enabled milliners like Rose Bertin, ruined by the wholesale flight from the city of her best customers, to earn at least a modest living.

Cockades were made simply from straight pieces of ribbon. Coloured fabrics, however, enabled the whole body to be dressed in the three colours. Red waistcoats and white stockings with blue clocks were available to men; women had skirts and *caracos* striped in blue, white and red, and white shoes with tricoloured rosettes. Women could also buy coats in 'national' blue (the blue worn by guardsmen) with a scarlet collar; these could rapidly have been transformed into uniform coats had Théroigne de Méricourt implemented her idea of raising a female regiment, as she threatened.

The colour red soon began to prevail in the militant sections, whose members were known as the *sans-culottes* because they adopted working men's breeches. They also wore the *carmagnole*, a garment imported from the Italian town of Camargnola, where it was worn by

48. Pierre-Etienne Le Sueur, *Citizen arrested for not wearing a Cockade.*

labourers, and the famous red bonnet.[2] To judge by the examples of red bonnets now in the Musée Carnavalet in Paris, they were usually policemen's caps, with the point falling to one side of the face, rather than the classic *bonnet phrygien*. Only the facing was in red, embroidered in silk with allegorical scenes and mottoes, the rest being in dark blue or white woollen cloth. This uniform, worn by anti-establishment extremists, was never recognised by any of the revolutionary governments. Members of the successive revolutionary governments generally dressed with classic elegance in the tradition of their predecessors under the monarchy.

Although the colour green represented the Parisians in revolt at the time of the storming of the Bastille, and black signified support for the Third Estate, there were also colours worn by those in opposition to the Revolution. Monarchists flaunted a white cockade, which was considered highly provocative.

In 1789, when rioting broke out quite a number of citizens were already dressed in black following the death of the heir apparent, and their mourning assumed an additional nuance. In 1790 a few young aristocrats adopted the costume known as *demi-converti*; this was the half-mourning that symbolised their regret at losing their privileges and their resignation to the turn that events had taken. In 1791 the colours yellow and black had a symbolic meaning known only to the opposition. In 1792 the counter-Revolutionaries wore a gown *à la reine*, a hair-style *à la Louis XIV* or a bonnet *au bandeau royal*.

Whilst the public was expressing its approbation or rejection of the new ideas, political theorists were considering the different roles that costume might occupy (informative, functional, educational, aesthetic) in a new republic where all the structures of government were in the process of being rebuilt.

At first it seemed sufficient simply to do away with the institutions that had existed under the monarchy. Then the Constituent Assembly refused to go on wearing the uniform imposed on the States General by the king; a few days later the obligation to wear clerical dress was lifted.[3] In 1793 the tribunal of the sixth arrondissement requested the abolition of judges' uniforms and the Convention declared total freedom of dress for all citizens.[4]

It was at this point that the Société Populaire et Républicaine des Arts (with which the Convention had replaced the former Académie Royale), consisting at this period of a group of artists who were fervent republicans, began (between December 1793 and April 1794) to hold discussions on modes of dress. The outcome of these deliberations was a slim volume entitled *Considérations sur la nécéssité de changer le costume français*. This came into circulation on 22 April 1794 and eight hundred copies were delivered to the Assembly.

The Société Populaire et Républicaine des Arts considered that costume should respect the requirements of hygiene and should protect the body without causing it harm; it should be loose enough to permit women to give birth to normal babies. It should respect all freedoms, not only allowing freedom of movement, but also abandoning any inappropriate shapes that 'frivolous despots' might try and impose upon it. It should also respect equality: it should distinguish neither rank nor fortune, and should therefore be the same for all citizens including soldiers, who would be armed only when occasion demanded. It should co-operate in the propaganda effort by making the French stand apart from those people still 'condemned to servitude'. Above all it should not conceal the beautiful shape of the body, nor frustrate the inspiration of artists preparing to immortalise brave warriors or the sublime splendours of the Revolution. In other words, for these men, all of whom had received a classical education, only one item of clothing, a garment closely based on classical dress, could possibly live up to what was expected of it.

The *Considérations* certainly had something to do with the decision taken by the Committee on Public Health on 25 Floréal, Year II (14 May 1794) to appoint the painter Jacques-Louis David to present 'his opinions and ideas on ways to improve costume as it is at present and to adapt it to republican moral standards as well as to the character of the Revolution'. In June, the artist, who had been appointed arts minister and was currently exerting his influence on a whole generation of art students, delivered his suggestions. His famous series of drawings, engraved by Vivant-Denon, includes designs for military costume, costumes for judges, municipal officers, representatives of people in the armed forces, representatives of civil servants, legislators, clothes for the French civilian population and informal wear for French citizens.

The collection of designs shows clearly that the artist had tried to establish a compromise between supporters of the single uniform for everybody and those who, like the Legislative Assembly, had realised that it was necessary for civil servants to wear distinctive clothing to indicate the type of authority that was vested in them. The same spirit of compromise can be observed in the various sources for David's designs. Antiquity, of course, the most important iconographic source for artists at the time, was evoked by the mantle worn by the People's Deputy, the tight hose suggesting heroic nudity of the legs, and the boots resembling classical buskins. The Middle Ages were represented too: the sash draped from the headwear of a municipal officer recalled the headdress of a fifteenth-century chaperon. The garment resembling a *simarre* with full sleeves worn by the representative of the armed forces could have been inspired by the doublet of François I. The legislator's cloak, full and with cone-shaped half-sleeves, is closely related to the long gown worn by the legal profession; the flat hats also bear a resemblance to the magistrates' mortars. The tunics worn by all David's figures are not too distant in style from contemporary dress, the main difference being that they fasten down the front rather than towards the back. David's designs show an eclectic taste and a tendency towards romanticism of which perhaps he himself was unaware.

The Société Populaire et Républicaine des Arts was not the only body concerned with costume. In his *Fragments d'institutions républicaines*, Louis de Saint-Just proposed the wearing of distinctive clothing according to age and position in society. An anonymous piece sent to the Committee for Public Education recommends the adoption of national dress by citizens as they pass from childhood into adulthood and acquire their rights. On 13 July 1793, bearing in mind the position of children too young to have been corrupted by society under the Ancien Régime, Robespierre proposed, as he presented the education plan prepared by Le Peletier de Saint Fargeau, that children should wear a uniform from the age of five in order to accustom them to equality.[5] During the debate that followed, Citoyenne Clemenceau replied by advocating a practical costume made of thick cloth in the national colours.[6] Two years earlier a Dr J.B. Faust had submitted another plan to the legislative body. This consisted of a 'free, uniform and national garment to be worn by children'. The plan contained a mixture of the ideas of Jean-Jacques Rousseau on the freedom of the body and contemporary ideas on the 'liberty of the soul'.

Apart from the military costume designed by David for students of the Ecole de Mars,[7] none of these proposals was ever adopted. The upheavals of Thermidor were approaching. Discussions on the matter of dress were not to be revived until after the voting for the constitution of Year III, when members of the future Directoire had to be equipped with uniforms.

Part Three

Chapter Twelve

Clothing and Accessories: Craft and Trades

In eighteenth-century France, craft and trades were still regulated by corporations whose powers were wide-ranging and strictly applied; production and professional training were closely monitored. In order for an aspiring tradesman to become a 'master' an apprenticeship had to be served, after which the apprentice became a *compagnon*. He then had to produce a 'master-piece' before he earned the title of 'master'. The sons of masters, on the other hand, had only to give evidence of 'experience'. A widow could continue to exercise the trade followed by her dead husband provided she did not remarry. Jurors, elected by each corporation, made regular visits to check that products were meeting the regulation standards: the slightest lapse would incur a penalty. Most of the statutes of the trade guilds of Paris, the oldest of which were collated between 1261 and 1265, were reviewed during the reign of Louis XIV and are still in force today. Owing to these arrangements a number of different trade corporations would be involved in the production of a single garment.

There were two types of guild, one for those responsible for the manufacture and finishing of goods and another for those responsible for selling the manufactured goods.

Using shuttle looms weavers produced fabrics of all kinds. The light linen fabric used for making underwear was woven mainly in Picardy, Anjou, Brittany and in Maine. 'Holland' was preferred for men's shirts. Coarse linen and hemp for making thick underskirts, paniers and the linings for whaleboned bodices were the speciality of Alençon, Mamers and Bolbec. Cotton weaving began in 1740 with the arrival of cotton from the French colonies in America, and was located in Rouen and Alsace.

Drapiers-drapans and *marchands-drapiers* made and sold all types of woollen cloth: drugget, flannel, flannelette, and ratteens and serge of pure wool or of wool mixed with silk, animal hair, linen or cotton. The master drapers of Paris numbered two hundred in 1770. They were still bound by the regulations of 1669, which determined the length and breadth of each piece of fabric and the width of its selvedges. The offices of the drapers' guild were in the Rue des Déchargeurs (its façade has been reconstructed in the Musée Carnavalet). Abbeville, Amiens, Elbeuf, Louviers, Reims, Rouen, Saint-Omer and Sedan were the main centres of the industry.

The manufacturers of cloth of gold and silver and of silk also made velvet – plain, cut and figured – satins, taffetas, moirés, corded silk, etc. measuring more than a third of an ell in width. The *tissutiers-rubanniers* made the same fabrics in narrower widths, as well as all kinds of ribbons, braids and trimmings. The term 'manufacture' did not mean that the enterprise was concentrated in large workshops. Labourers generally worked at home and would employ their wife and children to help raise the weft threads when they were making figured silks. In 1773 silk weaving in France made use of between twenty-eight and thirty thousand looms, spread between Lyon, Nîmes, Paris and Tours (the latter mainly devoted to furnishing silks); the ribbon-weaving industry in Saint-Etienne utilised twelve thousand looms.

The profession of dyeing was divided between the *teinturiers du bon teint*, who dyed fabrics, the *teinturiers en soie, laine, fil et coton*, who dyed yarn only, and the *teinturiers du petit teint,* who dyed everyday fabrics and gave new life to faded clothing. A fourth category appeared, the *imprimeurs sur étoffe* (fabric printers), when the activity of printing on cotton was officially authorised in 1759. Alsace, Paris and the Ile-de-France, Rouen and Normandy, Marseille and Provence, Lyon and the Dauphiné became the principal centres of the new industry – the first to bring large numbers of artisans together in comprehensive workshops.

The job of the *pelletiers-haubanniers* was to prepare and sell skins and leather. The *boutonniers-passementiers* produced and sold braid, buttons, beads and gold, silver and silk frogging; they also sold gold and silver lace, plain or with open work, pillow lace, bobbin lace and needle lace. A *boutonnier-passementier* had to serve five years as an apprentice and there were about 582 masters of the trade in Paris in 1779.

The *dentellières* (lacemakers), at any rate those that produced quality goods, owed the establishment of their profession in France to an edict of 1665 which stipulated that in the towns of 'Quesnoy, Arras, Reims, Sedan, Château-Thierry, Loudun, Alençon, Aurillac and others in the kingdom, manufactures of all kinds of thread work should be created: needle lace and pillow lace, and stitches like the ones practised in Venice, Genoa, Ragusa and other foreign places should be employed'. The ensuing thread work was henceforth known as *point de France*. In the eighteenth century the most important centres in France for lace were Argentan, Alençon and Sedan for needle lace and Valenciennes, Le Puy and Chantilly for bobbin lace. The lacemakers generally worked at home. In Valenciennes in order to find the correct degree of humidity for working with the thread they had to work in special cellars.

The *brodeurs-chasubliers* embroidered church hangings and vestments using gold, silver or silk thread, chenille or wool. The different kinds of embroidery executed by them were *broderie au passé*, which was reversible, *passé-épargné*, on the right side only, *broderie en nuances*, with shading to indicate relief and light, *en couchure*, with thick strands sometimes stitched flat to the fabric, *en guipure*, when gold is laid over a vellum wadding and stitched down with silk; *broderie en chaînette* was done with a needle, or, after 1760, with a hooked tool using a Chinese technique, and, finally, *broderie en rapport*, which was prepared separately on taffeta, tulle or paper and was then cut out and stitched on to the clothing. As well as women, quite a number of men were employed as lacemakers. *Broderie blanche* (whitework) was unrestricted and could be executed by anyone.

The *plumassiers* prepared and sold feathers for headdresses, clothing and for decorating certain items of furniture.

Apart from the people who actually made the goods, there were the *merciers*, people who 'sold everything and made nothing', as they

49. Charles-Germain de Saint-Aubin, *The Art of Embroidery*, 1770. Embroidery workshop.

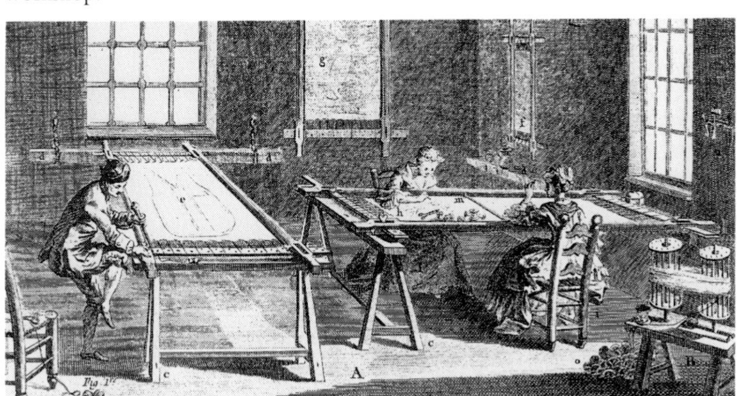

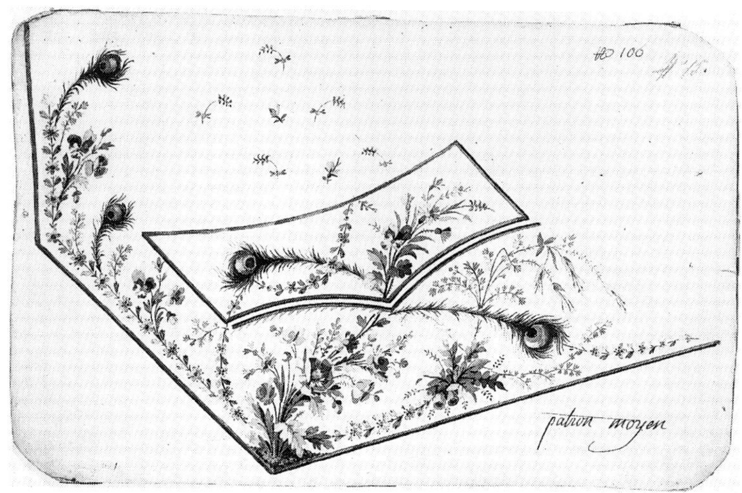

50. Painted pattern for embroidered waistcoat, 1780. Musée de la Mode et du Costume, Palais Galliera, Paris.

were then characterised; their role was rather similar to that of the department store today. They were divided into twenty classes or categories, some of them handling only clothes and accessories: lace, linen and muslin sellers, woollen cloth sellers, sellers of cloth of gold, silver and silk, ribbon sellers, sellers of gilt fringes and buttons and, lastly, sellers of small items of haberdashery (corresponding to the present-day haberdasher).

Finally, there were the people engaged in the making of clothes.

The *lingères*, as well as selling linen and hemp fabrics, batiste, lawn, canvas, net and lace, made linen underwear: shirts, collars, baby clothes and bridal trousseaux. They had to serve a four-year apprenticeship followed by two years of service before they could qualify as *maîtresses*. In 1725 the headquarters of the 559 'mistresses' of linen of Paris was in the convent of Sainte-Opportune.

The *tailleurs* or tailors of Paris, whose name derived from the word *taille*, meaning, in earlier times, both the cutting and the stitching of cloth, were governed by statutes dating back to 1660. For a long time they were the only category of tradesmen who dressed both sexes: besides making clothes for men, they retained the privilege of making trains (to be worn at court) and whaleboned bodices for women. Bodice-makers were specialists, *tailleurs pour femmes* or *tailleurs de corps de femmes et d'enfants* (fig. 18). A three-year apprenticeship had to be served, followed by at least three years' work-experience before the title of master could even be considered. It was prohibited to create more than ten masters per year, so that the number in Paris remained at approximately two hundred. Each master was allowed a maximum of one apprentice and six *compagnons*. All lived in, and food was provided. Their salary was in the order of four *livres* a month for the best workmen, and only three for the others. Day workers received only ten *sous* a day. The tailor was not licensed to sell fabrics and generally worked with fabrics brought by the customers; in fact, they sometimes charged their clients for material, paying the suppliers themselves. In 1671 Boulay published a large folio volume *Le Tailleur sincère*, devoted to the art of cutting cloth. A century later, Garsault brought tailoring techniques up to date in his *Art du tailleur*.

Couturières, who were originally seamstresses used by tailors and *lingères* to stitch seams, received authorisation in 1675 to make women's clothes (except for whaleboned bodices and trains), clothes for babies of both sexes and clothes for small boys up to the age of eight. They were permitted to make trimmings only if they were made of the same fabric as the dress. In 1782, in competition with the tailors, they gained the right to make bodices, corsets and paniers, men's dressing-gowns and the dominoes that were worn to balls. Their apprenticeship lasted three years, followed by two years in service. At the end of the eighteenth century there were about one thousand seven hundred *maîtresse-couturières* in Paris. Meetings of their guild were held in the church of Saint-Gervais. Their patron saint was St Louis.

The *marchandes de modes* made and trimmed hats, caps, *palatines*, fichus, mantelets and mantillas, that is, every garment that came into contact with women's heads and shoulders. They also made sleeves, belts and trimmings for dresses. They were originally dependent upon the *merciers*, but in Paris in 1776 they joined up with the *plumassiers-fleuristes*, who made flowers from feathers, and bouquets of artificial flowers for women.

Bonnetiers made and sold caps, stockings, bootees, gloves, camisoles, underpants and other items made on a frame or knitted in silk, wool, linen, cotton, beaver or any other yarn capable of being knitted. The first stockings to be made on a frame were executed in 1656 in the factory in the Château de Madrid, near Paris, on a piece of equipment made to designs brought from London by Jean Hindret. In 1751 Jean Berthier, mayor of Troyes, installed some knitwear frames in his town, establishing an industry that still prospers there today.

The *pelletiers-fourreurs* cut and crafted garments in fur: short capes and mantelets, muffs, linings for men's clothing and trimmings for ladies' gowns. The furs and skins most frequently used were beaver, squirrel, rabbit, marten, polecat and lamb. The most valuable furs came from Russia or Canada.

Chapeliers prepared wool, and beaver, hare and rabbit fur, and the fur of other animals that was suitable for felting to make hats.

Cordonniers made and sold boots, bootees and shoes; shoe repairs were the job of the *savetiers*.

Gantiers-parfumiers made and sold gloves made of leather, linen or silk, and these were generally perfumed. The apprenticeship lasted five years, followed by three years' work-experience. The 'masterpiece' required consisted of five exhibition pieces, cut and stitched.

Boursiers made the bags for bag wigs, black collars, umbrellas, parasols, breeches, game bags, cartridge pouches and other equipment for hunters.

Perruquiers made wigs and were men's hairdressers. They formed a group with the *barbiers-chirurgiens* (barber-surgeons); ladies' hairdressers were admitted into the group in Paris in 1776.

This highly complex corporate structure guaranteed quality for the consumer, but was a hindrance as far as competition was concerned because it set limits on the numbers of master tradesmen and stifled initiative. The inventor of a type of 'half-beaver' hat, consisting of a layer of fur on a base of wool, had his enterprise closed from 1666 to 1734 because his product did not meet standards of quality – and this in spite of the insistent demands of his clientèle; he learned the hard way the danger of being inventive.[1] This explains the relatively slow speed at which fashions developed, particularly in the first half of the century, before the urge for innovation grew strong and the control exercised by the corporations relaxed somewhat.

In Paris the fashion trades were located in the Ile de la Cité, traditionally the centre of the luxury trade, and on the left bank of the Seine, in Rue Dauphine, Rue des Fossés-Saint-Germain and Rue du Four. They were even more prominent on the right bank, in Rue Saint-Antoine and in a rectangle bounded by Rue Saint-Martin, the Seine, Rue Croix-des-Petits-Champs and the boulevard. Rue Saint-Denis and Rue Saint-Honoré were commercially the busiest thoroughfares. According to the *Almanach Dauphin* of 1772, Rue

51. *Dressmaking, or Many Promises to Little Effect.* Engraving from the almanac *Les Belles Marchandes, Alamanach historique, proverbial et chantant*, 1784. Dressmaker's shop.

Saint-Denis housed fourteen *bonnetiers*, two embroiderers, three hatmakers, nine drapers, seven *lingères*, sixteen fashion houses, and sixty-eight mercers (not all of them, it must be said, specialising in clothing). The Rue Saint-Honoré, on the other hand, housed fifteen *bonnetiers*, three embroiderers, six hatmakers, three *couturières*, fifteen drapers, four *lingères*, thirty-four mercers, a glovemaker, ten furriers, thirteen tailors and twenty-one fashion premises, including that of Rose Bertin. This area certainly bore all the marks of a fashion district, located on the west side of Paris, with Mademoiselle Bertin as the forerunner of a *grand couturier*.

Rose Bertin started her career in the Rue Saint-Honoré but during the Revolution moved to Rue de la Loi, now Rue de Richelieu, remaining faithful to the area where she received her training under Mademoiselle Pagelle, dressmaker to the nobility. Bertin caught public attention when she made the wedding trousseau of the duchesse de Chartres, ordered from Mademoiselle Pagelle. There can be no doubt about Bertin's talent; without it she would not have remained at the head of her profession for thirty years. She was possessed of a fertile imagination, as is proved by the enormous variety of head-dresses (no two were the same) and trimmings that she created, and an unusual talent as a business woman. The intelligent manner in which she exploited her good fortune when the duchesse de Chartres introduced her to the princess royal; the influence she was able to acquire over the young queen; her knack for self-publicity when she talked loudly of 'her work with the queen', when she stood on her balcony with her seamstresses to wave at the royal party as they came into Paris; when she hung portraits of Marie-Antoinette and the comtesse du Nord in her salons; her sense of her own importance and the haughty way she dealt with people judged to be unworthy of being clothed by her, whilst acting in a friendly and attentive manner towards anyone who might obtain flattering orders for her; the exorbitant prices she charged until her bankruptcy in 1787 – probably simulated in order to obtain money owed to her by the royal exchequer: all of this suggests a character well equipped to cope with life's struggles. With her twenty workers she represented a considerable business, able to dictate its own rules – the rules of Paris fashion – to all the courts of Europe. Her activity, nevertheless, could never step beyond the social organisation of the day. The fact that a *marchande de modes* – rather than a dressmaker or tailor – could achieve such eminence illustrates both the restrictive role played by the corporations and Bertin's ability to exploit the loopholes inherent in the status of *mercier*, one who 'sells everything'. The lists of her suppliers in 1790, 1791 and 1792, after the abolition of the trade corporations, include tailors, dressmakers and embroiderers. She was evidently sub-contracting some of the sewing work to tradesmen outside her own business.

The fame of Rose Bertin should not overshadow other talented craftsmen (and women) of the period, in particular Valentine and Beaulard whom she managed to oust from their premier positions (Beaulard never forgave her; he obliged Madame d'Oberkirch to listen for a whole hour while he ranted and raved against a rival who, he claimed, 'had the airs and graces of a duchess although she wasn't even remotely middle class').

In the queen's service were also Demoiselle Moulart and Madame Eloffe, successor to her aunt, Madame Pompey, the *marchande de modes* in Versailles; there were tailors too – Smith, Pujols, Taillade and Lespinasse, who were in charge of bodices and trains and of the queen's riding clothes.

The king's ceremonial costumes were made by Dargé, the master tailor of Paris, cut from silk obtained from Lenormand or Gibert in Rue des Bourdonnais, or from Martin or Barbier and Tétard. Leduc, another tailor, took care of the king's woollen clothing, purchasing cloth from Cuvillier Frères or from Quatremer in Paris, or ordering it direct from Elbeuf or Louviers. Vanot in Rue de Grenelle supplied linens and lace. Thélier and Madame Benoist were in charge of embroidery when this was not applied to the fabric in advance.

The almanachs list the names of several other suppliers to royalty or to the ladies of the court.

The *fripiers* or second-hand clothes dealers had quite a different clientèle, but were just as important at a period when no ready-made clothing was available at all (only a Mr Dartigalongue advertised ready-made clothing for clients, in 1770). Otherwise, the only way of buying ready-made clothes was to buy them second hand. In a country like France, and particularly in a city like Paris where rich and poor alike tired quickly of their finery, the second-hand clothes trade flourished. In order to re-stock their wardrobes some sold and others gladly bought, at prices lower than they would have paid if they had had recourse to the services of a dressmaker or a tailor. The second-hand clothes shops in Paris were under the arches of Les Halles. They were so ill-lit that customers sometimes received nasty surprises. 'You think you have bought a black coat but in broad daylight you see that it is green or purple and spotted like a leopard skin', complained Louis-Sébastien Mercier in the *Tableau de Paris*. He also mentioned a very fashionable market, the Foire du Saint-Esprit, that took place every Monday in the Place de Grève.

> Small townswomen, procuresses and over-thrifty women go there to buy caps, gowns, *casaquins* and cloth, even ready-made shoes. This market contains the jumble of a whole province, the spoils of a population of Amazons. Skirts, full petticoats, informal dress, all

scattered around in heaps from which you can make your selection. Look, the procuress is buying a gown that used to belong to the dead wife of a judge; that grisette is trying on a cap that belonged to the chambermaid of a *marquise*. In the evening the whole collection of old clothes disappears as if by magic. Not a cape or gown is left, and yet this inexhaustible supply will reappear promptly on the following Monday.

Chapter Thirteen

The Price of Elegance

It is difficult to assess the value of the *livre* in the eighteenth century in relation to the money of today. In the previous chapter we learned that the monthly salary of a working tailor was 4 *livres*. In 1792, women workers in the fashion trade who did not have their own outlet earned 450 *livres* per year, but Daniel Roche described these as forming 'the aristocracy of wage earners'. It is disappointing to have to acknowledge the fact that the old bills have little meaning nowadays. Nevertheless, they still provide a scale of labour costs. The outlay made by men and women of fashion on fabrics and on embroideries involving gold, silver and precious stones was often enormous; labour costs formed a very small fraction of their budget, and it is for this reason that it is interesting to look at contemporary invoices.

A series of bills now in the Musée de la Mode et du Costume in Paris reveal that a Mademoiselle Gaillard, a seamstress in Paris who made clothes for Madame de Bercy de Conflans for twenty years, charged her client 6 *livres* for the making of a dress in 1735. The fabric was always provided by the customer, and Mademoiselle Gaillard's price was the same whether the fabric was white corded silk, cerise drugget, blue and silver taffeta, sprigged gauze, Persian silk with a white background or a pink shot taffeta. Evidently, all the dresses were cut to the same pattern, which was probably a *robe volante*. The price for making up remained steady. In 1756 making an outfit still cost 6 *livres*, but this was for the overgown only, because the *robe à la française* was much more complicated to make than the *robe volante*. The bills record the appearance of a petticoat 'matching the dress' in 1737. In 1742 and 1743, for 7 *livres* each, dresses were accompanied only by a *tablier* (apron). From 1745 the petticoat and *tablier* were always mentioned in the bill and cost 2 *livres* each; trimmings began to make their appearance ('two borders on the fronts', the underskirt 'patterned'), requiring '4 ells of braid', and the attaching of the trimmings by the seamstress cost 8 *livres*. For the same amount of money the trimmings on the front of the dress were sewn on, and the underskirt was decorated with 'a small and a large flounce with the gap filled'. From 1750 stomachers are mentioned, 'hooked or buttoned' or as *compères*; these cost three *livres* if time had been spent trimming them, or 1 *livre*, 10 *sols* if they were left plain. Finally, in 1756, on a gown of 'thick Tours silk, white with multicoloured flowers on it' the dressmaker added (for an additional 10 *livres*), an 'elaborate trimming' which required 36 ells of braiding *à la reine*, at a cost of 14 *livres*, 8 *sols*. The price of an outfit had increased from 6 *livres* to an average of 12 *livres* over twenty years, but this was simply because the number of components had increased.

In 1756 Mademoiselle Gaillard was replaced by Madamoiselle Saulmont, who continued to dress Madame de Bercy until 1769. Her prices were low: a *robe-jupon* cost only 8 *livres* to have made.

The prices charged by tailors were fairly stable too. In 1739, according to invoices in the Palais Galliera, Monsieur La Borde was charged 40 *livres* for having a coat, a waistcoat and two pairs of breeches made, whether the garments were made of silk drugget, a *camelot*-silk mixture or velvet; 15 *livres* for an overcoat and breeches in grey wool, 9 *livres* for a dressing-gown with matching waistcoat, in floral material from India. Ten years later, Monsieur de Cramayel paid Michel, a tailor of Paris, 8 *livres* for a dressing-gown and a waistcoat in flowered satin. It cost no more than 18 to 24 *livres* to have a whole outfit made up. In 1782, however, Louis XVI paid Mutrel only 12 *livres* for making his frock coats, 6 *livres* for each pair of breeches and 6 *livres* for his waistcoats, but he paid Dargé, who made ceremonial clothing for him, from 30 to 45 *livres* for a suit of three pieces and 24 *livres* for suits comprising only a coat and a waistcoat; breeches cost 8 *livres* and separate waistcoats 10.

All these prices are exceedingly low when compared with the price of fabrics. In 1782, it is true, the woollen cloth worn by Louis XVI – scarlet for the parade ground, blue for hunting to hounds, green for shooting, grey for the coat he wore in the mornings before his first public appearance – cost respectively 25 *livres*, 10 *sols*; 24 *livres*; 20 *livres*; and 28 *livres* the ell. Even silks, although they were slightly narrower than the wool and between 8½ ells and 9 ells were needed to make a complete outfit (instead of 4½ ells of Holland ratteen) were reasonably priced at 14 to 20 *livres* the ell. But prices greatly increased when cloth of silver or gold was required, or elaborate embroidery.

The written records relating to the wardrobe of Louis XVI, in the Archives Nationales in Paris provide the total cost of some of his outfits. A complete suit of clothes in lilac watered silk, embroidered with silver and precious stones, with frogging, was delivered on 19 May 1782 by Dargé, who charged 45 *livres*, 15 *sols* for making it up; he required 8½ ells of fabric at 14 *livres* per ell (119 *livres*); two and a half dozen large silver buttons embroidered with white diamonds and green and lilac sequins, at 21 *livres*, 20 *sols* per dozen (52 *livres*, 10 *sols*); and two dozen small buttons at 10 *livres*, 10 *sols* per dozen (26 *livres*, 15 *sols*). Embroidering the coat in silver with precious stones cost 1,400 *livres*. The whole outfit cost 1,642 *livres*.[1] On 25 December 1781 Leduc delivered a suit to the king to wear for his triumphal entry into Paris. The tailor charged 221 *livres*, 26 *sols* for making up and for some of the materials, but the silver fabric (gold for the waistcoat and trimmings) cost 4,350 *livres*; the all-over embroidery (a mosaic of gold, silver, blue sequins and pink pearls), plus the silver embroidery (also all over) cost 2,800 *livres*. With the buttons, the outfit eventually cost more than 7,400 *livres*.[2]

The same sort of prices were paid by women, who would buy the 18 or 20 ells of fabric required to make a 'dress on a panier', or an equivalent length decorated in advance, and hand the material over to a dressmaker.

In 1772 Madame du Barry collected from Le Normand, dressmaker in the Rue Saint-Honoré, 'a formal dress, with boned bodice, white satin with garlands of roses embroidered on it, the roses with bows of pink, gold and silver sequins. The border goes round the *bas de robe* (the train) and the skirt'. She paid 5,600 *livres* for the gown, plus 240 *livres* for additional embroidery in gold sequins. In June the following year she bought three dresses in white grogram, also from Le Normand; one was embroidered with garlands and separate bunches of flowers and embroidered over with large and small sequins; it cost 6,000 *livres*. The cheapest cost 3,260 *livres*. Finally, in October, she acquired two formal outfits to wear at court, one in pink and silver satin with a boned bodice embroidered in silver, embroidered over with large and small sequins enamelled in pink and with a garland embroidered round the hem. This cost 7,600 *livres*. The other was in white velvet with multicoloured enamelled sequins all over the bodice, and a handsome border around the skirt and the train, all matching; this cost 12,000 *livres*.

These figures confirm that it was the cost of the fabrics that made clothes expensive. The bills also reveal the care that people took to make their clothes last. Madame de Bercy had her clothes mended and sometimes even re-made. For 10 *livres* Monsieur de Cramayel had one of his red woollen coats altered for his valet and, when the fashion changed in 1769, had the sleeves of a grey wool coat shortened. Madame du Barry took a formal dress of silver lamé to Le Normand to have the rust cleaned off it; Le Normand charged her 96 *livres* for doing the job. When Louis XVI's girth increased, his clothes were not replaced, they were simply let out.

Even the queen herself had the gauze of her fichus replaced and had some of her dresses mended. The clothes in museums bear witness to the use and re-use of fabrics: the fabrics of some *robes à l'anglaise* in museum collections show clear traces of pleats, which means that these were originally *robes à la française* that were altered according to changing fashion.

The invoices of the *marchandes de modes* are often more enigmatic than those of the *couturières* because of the difficulty of distinguishing the price of making up from the price of materials. When, in 1734, Madame Duchape sent Mademoiselle de Baudry a bill for 24 *livres* for making up an outfit in embroidered gauze, trimmed with *souci d'anneton nué* and also 'sprigged with matching bunches of flowers', it is obvious that the payment was for her work (sewing on the trimmings). The same was true when she charged 3 *livres,* 10 *sols* for 'making a bodice-piece' (a stomacher) and a fichu. However, when in 1773 Mademoiselle Pagelle sent Madame du Barry a bill for 10,300 *livres* for trimming a court gown, the sum obviously included the sewing and all the materials for the 'garlands of sable and roses, the net to support the garlands, arm garters, beads and *palatines*' that ornamented the whole *toilette.* Mademoiselle Bertin's bills were similar to these and the comptrollers at Versailles reproached her for not itemising them clearly. Because of their business links with the mercers these women had a tendency to sell their trimmings as ready-made pieces. They also sometimes behaved like contractors, paying the seamstress, the embroiderer, the sleeve-maker, the panier-maker or the diamond-setter directly and passing the various invoices on to the customer.

Fortunately, Madame Eloffe took the trouble to make a note of the price of fabric per ell and the cost of the number of ells purchased, and the cost of her labour. Thus it is learnt that between 1787 and 1789 the price of making a formal gown was about 15 *livres* and the price of making a simple *robe à l'anglaise* was about 3 *livres*, which is very little.

Hats also were sold by *marchandes de modes* and prices varied, probably according to both the dimensions of the hat, fashions for which changed from year to year, and the renown of their designer. In 1747 a gauze cap trimmed with ribbons could be obtained for 3 *livres* from a Mademoiselle Path. This was probably one of those small hats people wore perched on top of their head at that period. Forty or so years later Rose Bertin, the most respected milliner in Paris, sold a mourning headdress made of crape for 36 *livres*, a half-cap of gauze and silk bobbin lace for 48 *livres* and a bonnet *en cauchoise* (probably very tall like the headdresses worn by peasant women in the Pays de Caux) in gauze and beautiful silk bobbin lace with a satin ribbon for 60 *livres*. In 1787 fashionable hats bore more resemblance to hot-air balloons than to little lace butterflies. Poufs were very fashionable at the time; these usually consisted of a length of gauze draped in a ring with a flounce of silk lace plus a few frills and furbelows. The price of these (still from Rose Bertin) was between 86 and 120 *livres*, the difference probably being accounted for by the number of feathers used to trim the hat: 86 *livres* for a pouf with three feathers, 96 for a pouf with four feathers, 120 for a pouf with three good white feathers and an aigrette. Hats made in 1778 with trimmings of various kinds cost between 36 and 48 *livres* from Rose Bertin and between 20 and 33 *livres* from Madame Eloffe. Once again it is difficult to discover the cost of the labour and that of the materials, but materials accounted for a large part of the total amount.

The economics of underwear were similar. Madame du Barry bought linen at 3 *livres* the ell to make some shirts, and batiste at 9 *livres,* ten *sols* to trim them with. She also bought plain muslin at 8 *livres* the ell to make a petticoat. Making the shirts for her little black page, Zamor, cost 1 *livre* each, and making a dozen handkerchiefs 1 *livre*, 6 *sols* for the whole lot. However, she paid from 3,500 to 4,000 *livres* for house coats in *point d'Angleterre*, and from 3,000 to 5,740 *livres* for lace trimmings, including a barb for court wear, six rows of *engageantes* (layered lace ruffles), also for wearing at court, and a neckerchief in *point d'Argentan* or needle lace. The value of the lace determined the price of a garment. The lacemaker received only 18 *livres* for her work on the undersleeves of a formal court gown.

This illustrates the disproportion existing between labour costs and the price of some of the luxury materials then in use, and the disproportion between wages and what was paid for outfits costing 8,000 to 10,000 *livres*.

CHAPTER FOURTEEN

The Dissemination of Fashion

UNDER THE ANCIEN RÉGIME, the task of promoting and publicising fashion, nowadays carried out by models, was entrusted to dolls. This procedure dated back to the Middle Ages: in the first recorded example in 1391, Queen Isabeau of Bavaria sent a doll, for which she paid the court embroiderer 459 *livres,* to her daughter Isabel, the queen of England. Isabel was already an adult, so the doll must have been a fashion model. Later, in 1496, Anne de Bretagne commissioned a clothed doll with its hair done in the latest style to be sent to Isabella of Castille. When Henri IV was betrothed to Marie de Médicis, he used to send her *poupines* to show her what French fashions were like. Up to this point, fashion dolls were extravagant but occasional royal gifts.

Private individuals became involved in the spread of fashion during the seventeenth century. It is possible, however, that, owing to the misinterpretation of a document, the role in the matter attributed to Madeleine de Scudéry may have been misunderstood. What is not in any doubt is the fact that two dolls, a large and a small Pandora, one dressed in ceremonial dress and the other informally, were sent back and forth on a regular basis to recipients in France and abroad. In 1703 and 1713, during the war of the Spanish Succession, the aggressors, France and England, had an agreement that these fashion emissaries should be permitted to cross the battle lines.[1]

In the eighteenth century veritable circuits were set up. Dolls from Paris were exhibited at the Feria Franca in the Piazza San Marco in Venice. In 1712 an English newspaper published the news that 'on Saturday last the French doll for the year 1712 arrived at my house in King Street'. In 1739 the President des Brosses noted that large dolls dressed in the latest fashion were being sent to Bologna daily from Paris. In 1788, Deisbach confirmed that dolls were ordered from Paris 'so that women could have the dolls' clothes imitated by their own dressmakers'.[2] Rose Bertin was far too shrewd to overlook this means of advertising her wares; the result was that, all over Europe, the doll from the Rue Saint-Honoré was eagerly awaited, whether it had been sent for by wealthy customers or was being sent through the usual commercial channels.

The appearance of these dolls has long been a matter for speculation. Were they full-size models, or were they the size of a children's plaything, as were the dolls made for the same purpose during the Second Empire? An invoice from Madame Eloffe for a fashion doll, sent to the comtesse de Bombelles on 18 August 1788, may provide an answer to this question.[3] This was a doll in full court attire. The doll, supposedly in its clothes, was packed in 'a very large box' with a reinforced base, which certainly suggests that it was larger than a child's plaything. The doll's skirt, requiring two ells of white satin, was worn over a panier; the train measured two and a half ells, but these measurements do not correspond to normal adult measurements. In this instance, at least, it appears that the object was a large but not adult-sized doll; full-sized mannequins were already being used in shops at this time.

The National Museum of Monaco acquired a small wooden doll, which may be a fashion doll, with the collection of Madame Galéa. It is very rustic in style and its gown, petticoat and hat, faithful imitations of the garments worn by a fashionable adult in about 1778, can easily be removed.

By 1788 fashion dolls were enjoying their final moment of glory. Three years earlier the fashion magazine, illustrated with engravings, made its first appearance in France (it had already existed in England for eighteen years), and it soon supplanted the fashion doll. It was much simpler to circulate sheets of paper that packed flat and weighed little than to circulate a three-dimensional object that was bulky, fragile and expensive.

Published magazines were long preceded by fashion plates, singly or in series. In the eighteenth century there was a series by Watteau, *Figures de différents caractères*, engraved by Audran, and one by Boucher, *Recueil des différents modes du temps*, engraved by Truchy and Grignon, and *Douze figures de mode* which Boucher engraved himself after drawings by Dandridge. In 1750 six fashion drawings by Augustin de Saint-Aubin, engraved by Gilbert, appeared. Then there were six fashion plates engraved by Louise Gaillard, three after Schenau and three after P.A. Wille, and finally the *Suites d'estampes pour servir à l'histoire des moeurs et du costume des Français dans le* XVIIIe *siècle*, by Freudeberg and Moreau le Jeune. This series was better known as the *Monument du Costume physique et moral de la fin du XVIIIe siècle*; a new edition was published as such in 1789 with text by Restif de la Bretonne.

The public had also given an excellent reception to the new almanachs, small-sized books containing advice and news of all kinds, with some fashion plates. Shops used them to advertise their wares, and as many as forty or fifty thousand copies of some editions, designed to be given as presents at Christmas or New Year, were printed.

Of all these publications, the *Galerie des Modes et Costumes français dessinés d'après nature* was one of the most important because it came out at regular intervals and appeared for a number of years, which gave it close resemblance to a fashion magazine. It was published from 1778 onwards by Esnauts and Rapilly from premises in Rue Saint-Jacques, at the sign of the town of Coutances. Each edition originally comprised a folder of six prints, each print presenting four hats; from the seventh edition onwards full-sized figures were illustrated. The *Galerie des Modes* appeared at irregular intervals, in fact, and publication ceased in 1787. Respected draughtsmen including Claude-Louis Desrais, Pierre-Thomas Leclerc, François-Louis-Joseph Watteau, Augustin de Saint-Aubin were employed. The plates were produced by engravers of the calibre of Nicolas Dupin and his son Jean-Pierre-Julien, Adrien Lebeau, Etienne-Claude Voysard, Charles-Emmanuel Patas, Pierre-Charles Bacquoy, A. Duhamel, Le Roy, Aveline, Pélissier, Le Bas, Janinet, Wossenick. The engravings were published in black and white and in colour.

In December 1779 the first sixteen folders were gathered together in one volume with a frontispiece, introduction, description of the plates and reproduction of the copyright. A second volume appeared in 1780 containing the next ninety-six plates, with a foreword and a description of the clothes. The text in both volumes was by Guillaume-François-Roger Molé, lawyer to the booksellers and author of historical essays on Paris fashion.

The *Galerie des Modes* had its imitators in Paris and abroad, some more skilful than others; there were also counterfeiters who, by law, had to be prosecuted. It was a series of photographs rather than a true periodical. On 17 November 1785, however, the first issue of the *Cabinet des Modes* appeared, published by the bookseller Buisson, which after a year became the *Magasin des Modes nouvelles françaises et anglaises* and cost thirty *livres* a year: each octavo page was illustrated

52. Anonymous, *Cabinet des Modes*, 15 November 1785. The first published plate.

with three plates, and a notice advertising its appearance twice a month was included, though this time-scale was not adhered to very strictly. This was the first French fashion magazine. It contained literary contributions as well, but it was the fashion plates that recommended it to the *marchandes des modes*, its most important market. A total of 388 plates was published (clothes, hats, carriages, furniture), engraved by Duhamel to designs by Desrais and Defraine, or, from 1787, from English publications. Between 17 November 1785 and 21 December 1789, when publication stopped, 132 issues appeared. In 1790 the magazine reappeared as the *Journal de la mode et du goût*, still published by Buisson, edited by Lebrun-Tossa; it managed to survive until April 1793, publishing three editions per month, each edition containing two engravings. By this time almost the whole of France was wearing working-class clothing and preoccupation with dress would have been out of place, except amongst those who were pressing hardest for its reform. Concern about fashion did not surface again until 1795, when it foundered in the extravagances of the Directoire.

Chapter Fifteen

Fashion and Literature

Inevitably, traces of the French national passion for fashion are to be found in the literature of the day. The imprint of seventeenth-century classical culture was still strong at the beginning of the eighteenth century: self-analysis was regarded with suspicion, with the result that interest in costume is to be found in the lighter genres such as correspondence, memoirs, diaries and comedies.

Novels of the period, even famous ones such as *Manon Lescaut*, by the Abbé Prévost, and Marivaux's *Marianne*, waste no time on description of dress; presumably they supposed that their readers were already familiar with it. Marivaux, as is well known, was not indifferent to elegance; the inventory of his well-stocked wardrobe proves this. He always describes the clothing of a well-dressed character as 'the handsomest in the world', without further detail. Evocative descriptions based on the author's own observation were not to come for another century, when the Romantic movement began to attach importance to individual responses. This is why historians of French dress have relied so heavily on Restif de la Bretonne, particularly on his *Contemporaines*, which abounds in details of clothing obsessively recorded by the author. Amorous (or pornographic) literature of the eighteenth century is full of interesting detail about different items of clothing and their use.

Throughout the Middle Ages and right up to the age of Molière, French comedy satirized excess of all kinds, including extravagances of fashion; this, however, was in plays that resembled modern musicals, rather than in classical drama, and on the whole the plays have not survived. Albert Franklin, the social historian, came upon popular works of this kind during his research and cited *Comédie des paniers* by Legrand, in which one of the characters marvels at the rate at which Parisian women change their appearance: 'The fair-haired ones become dark, the ones with bouffant hair styles now sport a head like a water spaniel, those who had whole belfries on their heads have curtailed their hair by a foot and a half, those who were as thin as a lath now have the girth of a watchtower.' This kind of joke about the whims of female fashion was an old chestnut that, in fact, never died out.

Le Mariage de Figaro was one of the most celebrated comedies of the period. It was famous because of the attitude towards contemporary morals and manners portrayed in it. The political and public stir it caused provoked a different kind of relationship to dress to that noted above. This time new styles in clothes and headwear were born, which members of fashionable society were desperate to obtain. Styles were given the names of characters in the play and figured in the *Galerie des Modes*. Beaumarchais describes in detail the way his characters are dressed: he says of the countess, 'her gown in the first, second and fourth acts is a comfortable *lévite*', and of Suzanne, 'her gown in the first four acts is a white *caraco* with basques, very elegant, with an elegant skirt and the kind of hat that has since been called by milliners "à la Suzanne" '. He also gives information about contemporary customs and habits throughout the play, providing modern historians with invaluable details on, for example, wedding hats ('a hat with a long veil, tall feathers and white ribbons'), or the habit women had of dressing 'with the aid of many pins'.

Letters, diaries and memoirs based on personal observation and the desire to inform are better sources of information. Writing commentaries on fashion was one of the favourite occupations in eighteenth-century salons, where *nouvelles à la main* were circulated and were later collected and printed. The chronicles of Louis-Sébastien Mercier (in which he tried to characterise Parisian life) and contemporary memoirs as well are full of interesting touches, sometimes full of approbation, sometimes critical, but always instructive. The memoir as a literary genre was particularly appreciated under the Restoration and flourished mainly in the nineteenth century, but these post-Revolutionary memoirs look nostalgically back to the caprices of fashion and the manners of the latter days of the Ancien Régime. Women paid particular attention to matters of dress, whether it was Madame Campan describing the '*robe à la française*, with pleats in the back and large paniers' which replaced the *habit de Marly* and continued to be worn until the end of the reign of Louis XVI, or Madame de Genlis dreaming of 'the glamour of a circle of about thirty well-dressed women, seated next to one another with their enormous paniers forming a rich trellis-work of flowers, pearls, silver and gold, of coloured paillettes and precious stones'.[1] The baronne d'Oberkirch recalls 'tiny flat bottles, curved to the shape of the head' which contained a small amount of water and were worn in the hair. These were worn with full court dress at the Trianon, where the queen was putting on a play. The marquise de la Tour du Pin vividly remembers the agony inflicted by 'straight heels, three inches high, which held the foot in the tip-toe position normally adopted for reaching the top shelf in the library'. Madame de Boigne records her gratitude at having been brought up in a fine cotton shift at a time when 'children were dressed like little ladies and gentlemen, and were so uncomfortable that they were grumpy and bad-tempered'.

Men did not totally eschew descriptions of clothing, particularly the comte d'Hézecques who described all the uniforms worn at Versailles when he was a page there. Comte Alexandre de Tilly draws a lively, witty portrait of the comte d'Escars: 'a short, tight coat, embroidered waistcoat, antique jewelled garters on breeches of a pale colour, shod from crack of dawn with little gold buckles on the arch of his foot, a small bag (colloquially known as a *crapaud* or 'toad') at the back of his neck, a fancy cane, wide-brimmed hat under his arm, pleated cambric neckerchief with a small bulls-eye diamond twinkling shyly from its folds, a blue sash bulging as his hand plays about under his coat, the rhythmical walk of someone on parade'.[2] Even François-René de Chateaubriand in his *Mémoires d'Outretombe* describes the contrasts in style of dress observed during the Revolution: 'Beside a man in *habit français*, with powdered hair, a sword at his side, hat under his arm, elegant shoes and silk stockings, there walked a man with short, unpowdered hair, wearing an English tailcoat and American neckerchief.'

These are the most vivid descriptions of contemporary society and its clothing. I myself have had such pleasure from my research into the literature, that I highly recommend it to anyone wishing to gain an idea of the way the French regarded costume and fashion in Age of Enlightenment.

Conclusion

At the beginning of this book, I pointed out how dress inevitably reflects the political, social and economic climate of the country where it is created and worn. To present the development of fashion without presenting it in its historical context would be to reduce an important chapter of history to a mere history of clothes.

Having traced the development of styles in a sequence that, out of context, might appear to be the product of sheer fantasy but that, in fact, is perfectly logical, and having situated this development within the experience of the various levels of the contemporary society, my conclusion is that the costume of eighteenth-century France attracts our interest because it reflects and elucidates a time of transition, a time at which all aspects of life were coming under scrutiny.

The desire for liberty was first displayed by the fashions of the Regency, at a court that had for decades been subjected to a form of royal cult by Louis XIV; court society now found that the demands made on it no longer matched its aspirations. The yearning for freedom increased as the century wore on, gradually influencing society at almost every level and culminating in a bid for equality that, in terms of clothes, led to the rejection of the sumptuary laws and finally to the reduction of social status (as manifested in dress) to a single level. The aristocracy contributed to the final levelling, as the Revolution approached, by seeking comfort and simplicity of attire, taking to the English manner of dressing because they were tired of formality. The working classes, frustrated by their lowly status and by poverty, showed themselves eager to imitate the elegant manner of dressing that had hitherto been restricted to courtiers.

From a technical point of view, the old-established trade corporations guaranteed excellent quality but made innovation impossible; just before the Revolution (when the corporations were abolished) they came under pressure, particularly from the *marchandes des modes*, who achieved numerous concessions and also a notoriety that pointed towards the way things would develop in the future. Dedicated to development of the opposite kind, the first factories were established at this time, initially to produce printed fabrics. Their output, reserved for some years for the well-to-do, soon produced radical changes in the appearance of the masses.

As far as inspiration is concerned, having abandoned the magnificence so cherished by Louis XIV in all the decorative arts, fashion was able to interpret the curves and counter-curves in vogue under his successor, and then the return to Antiquity and straight lines after 1750. At the end of the reign of Louis XVI fashion promoted the slashed sleeve and the Medici collar, borrowed from the sixteenth and seventeenth centuries, thus heralding a romantic trend whose development was thwarted by Revolutionary artistic doctrine, and had to wait for the Restoration to develop more fully.

The future, both close and distant – the yearning for liberty, the tendency towards egalitarianism, mass production and the Romanticism that was to be the ideal of a whole generation – was to be found in embryo in the fashion of the eighteenth century. Even court dress, in its most static and traditional aspects (barred from development by its close contact with the exercise of monarchical authority) was Napoleon I's main source of inspiration when he wanted to surround his newly acquired majesty with fitting accoutrements that had stood the test of time.

Apart from the prestige of traditional dress, mainly appreciated by members of the public who had previously had no access to it, the most striking feature of fashion of the late eighteenth century was the accelerating speed at which innovations began to appear. After forty years when the *robe à la française* had reigned supreme (or its working-class version, the skirt and pleated *casaquin*), suddenly, in rapid succession, there appeared in city circles the *polonaise*, the *circassienne*, the *robe à la turque*, then the *robe à l'anglaise*, the *redingote* and the *pierrot*. These were in fact the earliest examples of fashion as such, fashion in its current meaning of change for its own sake, without too much respect for tradition (which was by then considered the mark of a primitive society). Half a century later the fashion industry refused to take any more orders from the court, accepting directives only from its own specialists, the great dressmakers who themselves dictated to the court. Rose Bertin was the herald of their new role.

The fashion of the period to follow would of course rely heavily on the past – on techniques of weaving and embroidery not yet standardised by machinery, on the high quality of raw materials, used with a sureness of touch that could make a coat or a dress into a real work of art. These great advantages were gradually to disappear.

Notes

Introduction

1 'The king cut a charming figure', marquis d'Argenson. 'At the age of seventeen he was considered the handsomest young man in his kingdom', duc de Richelieu. Quoted in P. Lacroix, 1885, pp. 26 and 28.
2 M. Sarde, *Regards sur les Françaises*, Paris, 1985, p.404.
3 E. and J. de Goncourt, *La Femme au* XVIII*e siècle*, Paris, 1982, p. 291.
4 F. Boucher, *Histoire du costume en Occident de l'Antiquité à nos jours*, Paris, 1965, p. 191.

1 Clothing and Fashion

1 Montesquieu, *Lettres persanes*, Letter 99.
2 P. Lacroix, 1885, p. 475.
3 *Mercure de France*, October 1730. Quoted in A. Franklin, *Les Magasins de nouveautés*, vol. I, Paris, 1894, p. 274.
4 A. Franklin, *op. cit.*, p. 273.
5 'What hell our women have to go through, so tightly tied and bound that it sometimes produces great wounds on their ribs! Yes! They sometimes die of the wounds!' Montaigne, *Essais*, book I, chap. XL.
6 Princesse Palatine, *Correspondance*. Letter of August 1718. Quoted in A. Franklin, *op. cit.*, p. 279.
7 *Journal de l'avocat Barbier*, vol. II, March 1728, p. 37. Quoted in A. Franklin, *op. cit.*, p. 279.
8 A. Franklin, *op.cit.*, p. 276.
9 A. Watteau, *Pierrot content*, *La Partie carrée*, *L'Embarquement pour Cythère*. *Watteau*, exhibition at the Galeries nationales du Grand Palais, Paris 1984, nos 13, 14, 62, and Lancret, *La Leçon de musique*, Musée du Louvre.
10 *Mercure de France*, October 1730, p. 8.
11 *Exposition Subleyras*, Musée du Luxembourg, Paris, 1987, no. 63.
12 *Ibid.*, nos 5, 26, 27, 62.
13 *Boucher*, exhibition at the Galeries nationales du Grand Palais, Paris, 1986, no. 52.
14 *Id.*, no. 59.
15 The three panels are sometimes held to represent the division of Poland – the source of the gown's name. Proof of the dressmakers' imagination at the period are the variations on the *polonaise*: 'with spreading tail', '*en frac*', 'liberty style', 'with wings', 'with sleeves in the Circassian style', 'cut', '*à la Jean-Jacques*', 'two-ended'. Cf. *Galerie des modes et costumes français*, reprinted by P. Cornu, 1911, plates 10, 18, 21, 82.
16 Madame de Genlis, *Mémoires*, vol. VI, Paris, 1825, p. 195.
17 The *lévite* came into fashion in 1778, during Marie-Antoinette's first pregnancy. It was originally based on the costume worn by the Levites in the production of Athalie at the Comédie-Française. In 1781 the vicomtesse de Jaucourt caused a great stir with her 'monkey-tailed *lévite*'. Cf. *Mémoires secrets*, attributed to Bachaumont, 3 June, vol. XVII, p. 204.

18 It was created in Lyon in 1775. The *Galerie des modes et costumes français*, reprinted by P. Cornu, *op. cit.*, vol. I, plate 42, caption to the engraving.

19 *Dégradation de l'espèce humaine par l'usage du corps à baleines*, by Monsieur Bernard, 1770.

20 The *caraco* was a more fitted version of the *casaquin* and had been in use for longer. It was not until 1768, however, that the ladies of Nantes dared to wear the garment outside the house. Ten years or so later various versions were being made: *à la française, à la polonaise, à la dévote flottant, à la Pierrot*. Cf. *Galerie des modes et costumes français*, reprinted by P. Cornu, *op. cit.*, plates 12, 51, 58, 15, 28.

21 *Mercure de France*, 1726, p. 403.

22 'Indecent breeches, with no pockets, in which neither a coin nor a watch could be concealed'. Sébastien Mercier, *Le Tableau de Paris*, vol. X, p. 264.

23 A. Franklin, *Les Magasins de nouveautés*, vol. I p. 263.

24 From Carmagnola, the Italian town from which the wearers of this type of jacket originated.

25 A. de Garsault, *L'Art de la lingère*, 1771. 'The *maillot* is the name of the child's layette until it reaches the age of three.'

26 S. Boulanger, *La Vie quotidienne chez les ducs de Fitz'James au XVIIIe siècle*, Nanterre, 1971. Typed memoir. Quoted in F. Bluche: *La Vie quotidienne de la noblesse française au XVIIIe siècle*, Paris, 1973, p. 46.

2 Underwear

1 For information about body linen, see Garsault, *L'Art de la lingère*, 1771.

2 *Basin*, or dimity, was a twill cotton.

3 Jean Cordey, 'Inventaire des biens de Mme de Pompadour rédigé après son décès', *Société des bibliophiles français*, no. 1101.

4 A memoir in the Musée Galliera states that Michel, a tailor of Paris, made three 'pairs of cotton drawers' for M. de Cramayel in 1769.

5 J. Hubert, *Le Lever de Voltaire*, oil on canvas, Musée Carnavalet, Paris.

3 Accessories

1 *Livre-journal de Mme Eloffe*, 1885. The sleeves known as *maris* must have been made of fine lace and been worn under a frock coat or a *lévite* (invoices of 1787).

2 'A man without powder does not look well', Marivaux, *Romans*, 'Journal d'un Espagnol', Paris, 1966, pp. 868–9. Quoted in J. Meyer, *La Vie quotidienne en France au temps de la Régence*, 1979, p. 275.

3 The *Avant-coureur*, 2 November 1761, p. 696.

4 Musée Galliera, Inv. 1984-1-74.

5 May 1726, p. 950, quoted in A. Franklin, *Les Magasins des nouveautés*, vol. IV, Paris, 1894, p. 236.

6 Comte de Vaublanc, *Mémoires*, p. 139, quoted in A. Franklin, *op. cit.*, vol. IV, p. 240.

7 Vellum is a fine parchment used for painting; in this case used in fan making.

8 Baronne d'Oberkirch, *Mémoires*, Paris, 1979, p. 342.

9 Fan in the Musée Galliera collection. Cf. M. Leloir, 'Les Accessoires du costume, parasols et parapluies', in *Bulletin de la Société de l'histoire du costume*, no. 6, January 1909, pp. 129–37.

10 Carracioli, *Dictionnaire critique, pittoresque et sentencieux*, vol. II, p. 188. Quoted in A. Franklin, *op. cit.*, vol. IV, p. 323.

11 A. Franklin, *op. cit.*, vol. IV, pp. 324–5.

4 Fabrics and their Decoration

1 Fustian: oriental in origin, is a twill made of cotton and linen, or cotton and silk. Dimity: see chapter 2, note 2. Muslin: very fine cotton.
2 P. de Calan, *Le Coton et l'industrie cotonnière*, 1961, p. 82.
3 O. C. de Saint-Aubin, *L'Art du brodeur*, 1770, p. 30.
4 Wool fabric, sometimes mixed with silk and shiny on the right side.
5 Drugget: wool weft with cotton warp, squared or checked. *Dauphine* is like drugget but is not twilled.
6 *Pinchina*: a twill originally made in Spain. Rash: plain serge with a nap. A twilled serge, very warm, is named after the town of Sommières. *Revêche*: a coarse wool ratteen.
7 Velvet made by combining, on the same piece of fabric, cut velvet (the extra warp which is designed to be the pile is rolled over cutting blades) and pin velvet (the cutting blades are pulled out without cutting the pile).
8 *Passé* consists of embroidery with a thread on either side of the fabric, sometimes stitched over parchment or paper to give relief to the motif. It is called 'two-sided' if it has no knots visible and is reversible, or 'saved' if it covers only the right side of the fabric. *Chaînette* was made with a needle until 1760, when it began to be made with a hook following the Chinese procedure.
9 'Un album de modèles pour broderies de gilets', *Bulletin du Musée Carnavalet*, November 1956, 9th year, no. 2.
10 Paris, Musée Galliera, Inv. 1987-2-20. New York, Metropolitan Museum of Art, Costume Institute, Inv. 1983-1'208.
11 Musée Galliera, Inv. 1985-1-208.
12 *Id.*, Inv. 1985-1-163.
13 *Id.*, Inv. 1969-59-1.
14 *Id.*, Inv. 1986-68-1.
15 *Id.*, Inv. 1984-1-77, 1986-1-592, 1986-68-1.
16 *Id.*, Inv. 1984-1-77.
17 A.-M. Wiederkehr, 'Les dessinateurs lyonnais du XVIIIe siècle', *La soie*.
18 The improvement consisted of introducing a perforated card into the loom to make this operation automatic. The Falcon loom (1728) used a rectangular card, the Vaucanson loom (1746) a cylinder covered with card; only the Jacquart loom (1804) – which combined the two processes – was viable.

5 French Fashion, Europe and the East

1 Comtesse de Boigne, *Mémoires*, Paris 1986, vol. I, p. 35. 'I was not dressed in swaddling clothes, I was dressed in the English fashion.'
2 'Protestation d'un correspondant', *London Magazine*, 1738, quoted in F. Boucher, *Histoire du costume en Occident de l'Antiquité à nos jours*, Paris 1965, p. 323.
3 A. Ribeiro, *A Visual History of Costume. The Eighteenth Century*, London, 1983, p. 113.
4 *Four Hundred Years of Fashion*, Victoria and Albert Museum, p. 21, Court dress, about 1740.
5 *Ibid.*
6 F. Boucher, *op. cit.*, p. 326.
7 S. Flamand Christensen, 'De Danske kongers kronologiske samling paa Rosenborg', *Kongedragterne fra 17. og 18. aarhundrede*. 2 vols, Copenhagen, 1940.

6 Clothes for Special Occasions

1 A. de Garsault, *L'Art du tailleur*, 1769.
2 *Galerie des modes et costumes français*, reprinted by P. Cornu, 1913, plate 80.

3 S. Poignant, *Les Filles de Louis XV. L'Aile des princes*, 1970, p. 169.
4 *La Première Communion. Quatre siècles d'histoire*. Published by Jean Delumeau, Paris, 1987, p. 40.
5 J.-M. Gouesse, 'La communion solennelle à Coutances. XVIIe et XVIIIe siècles', *Revue du Département de la Manche*, fasc. 101–3 (actes du 18e Congrès des Sociétés historiques de Normandie), pp. 98–9.
6 J. Delumeau, *op. cit.*, p. 124.
7 L. Perrey, *Histoire d'une grande dame du XVIIIe siècle*, Paris, 1887. Quoted in J. Delumeau, *op. cit.*, p. 125.
8 E. M. Faillon, *Méthode de St-Sulpice dans la direction des cathéchismes*, Paris, 1832, p. 129. Quoted in J. Delumeau, *op. cit.*, p. 113.
9 F. Bluche, *La Vie quotidienne de la noblesse française au XVIIIe siècle*, Paris, 1973, p. 56.
10 A. Decaux, *Histoire des Françaises*, Paris, 1979, vol. II, p. 383.
11 Baronne d'Oberkirch, *Mémoires*, Paris, 1979, p. 265.
12 *Galerie des modes et costumes français*, reprinted by P. Cornu, 1913, plate 88 and *La Parure des dames*, Paris, 1779.
13 Baronne d'Oberkirch, *op. cit.*, p. 77.
14 Marquise de La Tour du Pin, *Mémoires d'une femme de cinquante ans*, Paris, 1979, p. 74.
15 *Ibid.*, p. 110.
16 *Ibid.*, p. 74. The trousseau offered to her by her grandmother cost 45,000 francs and comprised linen, lace and muslin dresses, but no silk dresses.
17 S. Mercier, *Le Tableau de Paris*, vol. I, chap. LXXVII, p. 246.
18 *Journal de l'avocat Barbier*, 13 March 1761. Quoted in A. Franklin, *Les Magasins des nouveautés*, vol. III, Paris, 1894, pp. 133–8.
19 I assume that the fabric alluded to was light, possibly fringed at the selvedges, suitable for making trimmings since it was used for the barbs on caps; after the mourning period it was replaced by brocaded silk gauze or by silk lace.
20 Black twill fabric, with a wool or linen warp, worn by widows and for full mourning.

7 Etiquette and Uniforms

1 For the costumes worn at the coronation, see Danchet, *Le Sacre de Louis XV dans l'église de Reims, le 25 octobre 1722*, large folio edition with 74 engravings, under the direction of the painter Dullin, Paris, 1722. Abbé Pichon, *Couronnement et sacre de Louis XVI*, engravings by Patas, Paris, 1775. The costumes were designed by Bocquet and executed by Delaistre, respectively the painter and the tailor attached to royal entertainments.
2 J -P. Bayard, *Le Sacre des rois*, Paris, 1964, p. 118.
3 Cf. *Ordres de chevalerie et récompenses nationales*. Catalogue to the exhibition at the Musée de la Monnaie, Paris, 20 March–30 May 1956, p. 51 *et seq*.
4 Cf. H. Vanier, *Les Costumes de l'Ordre du Saint-Esprit, à propos d'un manteau de chevalier conservé au musée Galliera*, in 'Bulletin du musée Carnavalet', 1971, no. 1.
5 Cf. *Ordres de chevalerie et récompenses nationales*, *op.cit.* p. 73 *et seq.*
6 A.-M. Passez, *Adélaïde Labille-Guyard*, catalogue raisonné, Paris, 1973, no. 101. *Réception d'un chevalier de Saint-Lazare par Monsieur, grand maître de l'Ordre*, sketch for a large painting destroyed during the Revolution, Paris, Musée de la Légion d'Honneur.
7 *Relation des cérémonies observés à l'occasion du mariage du Roy*, Paris 1725.
8 Costume (doublet, hose, belt and cloak) made by Monsieur d'Autran, tailor in ordinary to the King. Archives nationales, Inv. 3261.
9 A. Castelot, *Marie-Antoinette d'après des documents inédits*, Paris, 1953.
10 Comte d'Hézècques, *Page à la cour de Louis XVI*, Paris, 1987, p. 52.
11 *Ibid.*, p. 68.
12 Beneton de Morange de Peyrins, *Traité des marques nationales*, Paris, 1739 , p. 357.

13 For information about the pages and the guards, see Comte d'Hézècques, *op. cit.*, pp. 13, 14, 18, 24, 182, 184.
14 F. Bluche, *La Vie quotidienne de la noblesse française au XVIIIe siècle*, Paris, 1973, p. 239.
15 F. Bluche, *La Vie quotidienne au temps de Louis XVI*, p. 97. Quoted by marquis de Villeneuve Bargenon, 'Lettres d'un officier de l'Ancien Régime. Les honneurs de la cour', Carnets de la Sabretache, no. 267, 1920, pp. 257–84.
16 Marquise de La Tour du Pin, *Journal d'une femme de cinquante ans, 1778–1815*, Paris, 1951, p. 75.
17 M. de Decker, *Mme le chevalier d'Eon*, Paris, 1987, p. 212.
18 Baronne d'Oberkirch, *Mémoires sur la cour de Louis XVI et la société française avant 1789*, Paris, 1979, p. 89.
19 *Correspondance secrète*, attributed to de Bachaumont, 27 February 1785. The gown was also compulsorily worn to supper in the private apartments (cf. Comtesse de Boigne, *Récits d'une tante*, Paris, 1971, p. 37.)
20 Comte d'Hézècques, *op. cit.*, p. 89.
21 J. Levron, *La Vie quotidienne à la cour de Versailles aux XVIIe et XVIIIe siècles*, p. 115. The coat was worth between 800 and 1,200 *livres*.
22 See M. Gallet, *L'Ancien Hôtel de ville de Paris et la place*, Catalogue to the exhibition at the Musée Carnavalet, 1975.
23 R. Mesuret, *Les Enluminures de Capitole de 1610 à 1790*, Toulouse, Musée Paul Dupuy, 1956.
24 F. de Raiset, *Bordeaux au XVIIIe siècle*, 1968.
25 J. Dauviller, 'Les costumes des anciennes universités françaises', *First International Congress on the History of Costume*, Venice, 1952.
26 L. Trichet, *Le Costume du clergé*, Paris, 1986, pp. 133–43.

8 The World of Elegance

1 Comte d'Hézècques, *Page à la cour de Louis XVI*, Paris, 1987, p. 9.
2 Archives nationales, O/i 835.
3 P. Lacroix, *XVIIIe siècle. Institutions, usages et costumes*, France 1700–1789, Paris, 1885, p. 486.
4 Baronne d'Oberkirch, *Mémoires sur la cour de Louis XVI et la société française avant 1789*, Paris, 1979, p. 181.
5 Père de Larue, *Sermon sur le luxe des habits*, 1719, vol. I, pp. 239, 256. 'Luxury has ceased to be the vice of the nobility. We no longer need only to give lessons in modesty to people of that ilk; we need to give them to the working people and artisans.'
6 F. Bluche, *La Vie quotidienne de la noblesse française au XVIIIe siècle*, Paris, 1973, p. 70.
7 Madame Campan, *Mémoires*, Paris, 1988 (new edition), p. 23.
8 Madame Campan, *Mémoires*, Paris, 1823, p. 289.
9 Duc de Croÿ, *Journal inédit*, 1907, vol. IV, p. 53.
10 The sum was exceeded by 28,000 *livres* in 1776, 74,118 *livres* in 1780, 83,064 *livres* in 1783. See A. Castelot, *Marie-Antoinette d'après des documents inédits*, Paris, 1953, p. 155.
11 'We used to buy the clothes and formal coats to make furnishings'. Madame de Genlis, *De l'esprit des étiquettes de l'ancienne cour*, 1885, p. 47.

9 Clothes for the Working-Class

1 N. E. Restif de la Bretonne, *Mémoires*, published with the title *M. Nicolas*, 1770.
2 Marquis de Mirabeau, *L'Ami des hommes*, Paris, 1756.

10 Fashion and Current Events

1 The hair-style 'à la Belle-Poule', from *La Parure des Dames* (from a series of 12 plates in imitation of *La galerie des Modes*, published by Moudhare), 1779
2 *Galerie des modes et costumes français*, reprinted by P. Cornu, 1913, plates 116, 133.
3 *Ibid.*, pls 197, 303.
4 *Ibid.*, pls 188, 190, 197, 199 and 202.
5 *Ibid.*, pls 194, 195, 226, 315.
6 Musée Gilet, Paris, about 1780, inv. 62-108-385, coll. Galera.
7 *Magasin des modes nouvelles*, 1789.
8 *Journal de la mode et du goût*, July 1790.

11 Dress, Politics and Ideology during the Revolution

1 By royal decree of 19 May 1790.
2 See A. Soboul, *Les Sans-Culottes parisiens en l'an II*, Paris, 1968; M. Agulhon, *Marianne au combat, l'imagerie et la symbolique républicaines de 1780 à 1880*, Paris, 1979; A. Gérard, 'Bonnet phrygien et Marseillaise', in *L'Histoire*, no. 113, July–August 1988, pp. 49-50.
3 15 October 1789 and 24 October 1789.
4 7 Germinal, Year II and 8 Brumaire, Year II.
5 B. Baczko, *Une éducation pour la démocratie. Textes et projets de l'époque révolutionnaire*, Paris, 1982.
6 Archives nationales F. 17 1005 A, item 756.
7 The school was open from 20 Messidor, Year II (8 July 1794) to 2 Brumaire, Year III (25 October 1794).

12 Clothing and Accessories, Craft and Trades

1 A. Franklin, *Les Magasins des nouveantés*, vol. III, Paris, 1894, pp. 197–205.

13 The Price of Elegance

1 Archives nationales O/i835, items 297, 324, 315; 78.
2 Archives nationales O/i835, items 130, items 395, 329.

14 The Dissemination of Fashion

1 'During the furious hostilities engaged in by both sides, she (the doll) was the only thing respected by the weaponry'. Abbé Prévost, *Contes, aventures et faits singuliers*, Paris, 1784, p. 493.
2 Cl. Sezan, *op. cit.*, p. 99.
3 Comte de Reiset, *Modes et usages au temps de Marie-Antoinette, livre-journal de madame Eloffe marchande de modes ordinaire de la reine et des dames de sa cour*, vol. I, p. 268.

15 Fashion and Literature

1 Madame de Genlis, *Dictionnaire des étiquettes*, vol. II, p. 40.
2 Comte de Tilly, *Mémoires*, Paris, 1986, p. 530.

General Bibliography

Printed sources

Barbara Johnson's Album of Fashions and Fabrics (1746–1823), edited by Natalie Rothstein, London 1987.

Boigne, Comtesse de, née d'Osmond, *Récits d'une tante*, Paris, 1971.

Campan, Madame, first lady-in-waiting to Marie-Antoinette, *Mémoire sur la vie privée de Marie-Antoinette*, Paris, 1822, new edition 1988.

Galerie des Modes et Costumes français, dessinés d'après nature. . . ouvrage commencé en 1778. Published by Esnauts and Rapilly. The first volume with 96 plates appeared in December 1779 with an introduction of 40 pages by G.F.R. Molé, then a second in 1780. The folders of engravings then appeared separately until about 1787.

Gazette de la Reine pour l'année 1782. Facsimile of the register of the duchesse d'Ossun, edited by Pierre de Nolhac, Paris, 1925.

Garsault, François, *L'Art du tailleur*, 1769. *L'Art de la lingère*, 1771.

Genlis, Comtesse de, *Dictionnaire critique et raisonné des étiquettes de la cour et des usages du monde*, Paris 1818.

Mémoires inédits sur le XVIIIe siècle, Paris 1825, 8 vols.

Hézècques, Comte d', *Souvenirs d'un page de la cour de Louis XVI*, Paris, 1873, republished 1987.

La Tour du Pin, Marquise de, *Journal d'une femme de cinquante ans, 1778–1815,* Paris 1951.

Leroy, Alphonse, *Recherches sur les habillements des femmes et des enfants*, Paris 1772.

Oberkirch, Baronne d', *Mémoires sur la cour de Louis XVI et la société française avant 1789*, Paris, 1979.

Restif de la Bretonne, Nicolas-Edme, *Monsieur Nicolas*, Paris. *Les contemporaines*, 10 vols.

Saint-Aubin, Charles-Germain de, *L'Art du brodeur*, 1770. Facsimile edition, Los Angeles Country Museum of Art, 1983.

Savary des Bruslons, Jacques, *Dictionnaire universel de commerce*, 3 vols. The edition of 1741.

Tourzel, Duchesse de, governess to the royal children 1789–1795. *Mémoires*, Paris, 1969.

General Works

Aries, Philippe, *L'Enfant et la vie familiale sous l'Ancien Régime*, Paris, 1960.

Bluche, François, *La Vie quotidienne de la noblesse française au XVIIIe siècle*, revised and corrected edition, Paris, 1980.

La Vie quotidienne au temps de Louis XVI, Paris, 1980.

Chassagne, Serge, *Oberkampf, un entrepreneur capitaliste au siècle des Lumières*, Paris 1980.

Chaussinand-Nogaret, Georges, *La Vie quotidienne des Français sous Louis XV*, Paris 1978.

China und Europa, Chinaverständnis und Chinamode im 17. und 18. Jahrhundert, Berlin (Charlottenburg), 1978.

Franklin, Alfred, *La Vie privée d'autrefois, arts et métiers, modes, moeurs, usages des parisiens du XIIe au XVIIe siècle d'après des documents originaux ou inédits*, Paris 1890–1906. (*Les magasins de nouveautés*, 1895 – *La Vie à Paris sous Louis XVI, début du règne*: new edition of *La Quinzaine Anglaise* by Rutlidge, 1906.)

Goncourt, Edmond and Jules de, *La Femme au XVIIIe siècle*, Paris, Firmin–Didot, 1887. Edition introduced by E. Badinter, Paris, 1982.

Johansen, Katia, *Royal Gowns*, Copenhagen, 1990.

Lacroix, Paul, *XVIIIe siècle. Institutions, usages et costumes*, France 1700–1789, Paris 1885.

Lever, Evelyne, *Marie-Antoinette*, Paris, 1991.

Levron, Jacques, *La Vie quotidienne à Versailles au XVIIe et XVIIIe siècles*, Paris, 1978.

Louis XV, un moment de perfection de l'art français, Exhibition at the Hôtel de la Monnaie, Paris, 1974.

Madame de Pompadour et la floraison des arts, Montreal, David M. Stewart Museum, 1988.

Marie-Antoinette et sa cour, Bibliothèque de Versailles, 1927.

Marie-Antoinette archiduchesse, dauphine et reine, Château de Versailles, May–November 1955.

Meyer, Jean, *La Vie quotidienne au temps de la Régence*, Paris, 1979.

Costume and Fashion

Andersen, E., *Danske Dragter: Moden i 1700–årene*, Copenhagen, Nationalmuseet, 1977.

An Elegant Art: Fashion and Fantasy in the Eighteenth Century. Exhibition at the Los Angeles County Museum of Art, March–June 1983, Abrams, 1983.

Boehn, Max von, *Die Mode, Menschen und Moden im achtzehnten jahrhundert*, Munich, 1909, republished in London, vol. IV, 1935.

Boucher, François, *Histoire du costume en Occident de l'Antiquité à nos jours*, Paris 1965. Republished with additional material, 1988.

Buck, Anne, *Dress in Eighteenth-Century England*, London, 1979.

Coppens, Marguerite, *Le Costume au XVIIIe siècle*, Brussels, Musée royaux d'Art et d'Histoire, 1978.

Costumes français du XVIIIe siècle, 1715–1789. Musée Carnavalet, Paris, November 1954–January 1955. Notes by M. Delpierre.

Costumi del XVIII e XIX secolo, Palazzo Contronі-Pfanner, Lucca, 1980.

Delpierre, Madeleine, 'Costumes français du XVIIIe siècle', *Bulletin du Musée Carnavalet*, June 1962.

—— 'Robes de grande parure du temps de Louis XVI', *Bulletin du Musée Carnavalet*, no. 1, June 1966.

—— 'L'élégance à Versailles au temps de Louis XV', *Versailles*, no. 59, 1975.

—— 'Marie-Antoinette reine de la mode', *Versailles*, no. 59, 1975.

—— 'Petite chronologie d'une révolution dans la mode', *Modes et révolutions*, 1780–1804, Paris, Musée de la Mode et du Costume, Palais Galliera, 1989, pp. 9–39.

—— 'Les élégances de madame Du Barry', *Madame Du Barry, de Versailles à Louveciennes*,

Exhibition at the Musée Promenade de Marly-le-Roi-Louveciennes, March–June 1992, Paris, 1992, pp. 147–57.

—— et al., *Elégances du* XVIIIe *siècle, costumes français, 1730–1794*, Paris, Musée de la Mode et du Costume, December 1963–April 1964

—— et al., *English Costumes of the Georgian Period*, Los Angeles County Museum of Art, November 1957–March 1958.

—— et al., *Four Hundred Years of Fashion*, Victoria and Albert Museum, London, 1984.

Korchounova, Tamara, *Le Costume en Russie,* XVIIe *– début du* XXe *siècle*, Hermitage, Leningrad, 1983.

Leloir, Maurice, *Histoire du costume de l'Antiquité à 1914*, Paris, vol. X: Louis XIV, part 2 1678-1715 (1935) and XI: Louis XV 1725–1774 (1938) and vol. XII: Louis XVI and revolution, 1775–1795 (1949).

—— *Dictionnaire du costume de l'Antiquité à 1914*, Paris, 1951. New edition 1992.

Levi Pisetzky, Rosita, *Storia del costume*; vol IV: Il settecento, Milan, 1967.

Modes et Révolutions, 1780–1804, Musée de la Mode et du Costume, Paris, Palais Galliera, February–May 1989.

Pellegrin, Nicole, *Les Vêtements de la liberté. Abécédaire des pratiques vestimentaires en France de 1780 à 1800.* Aix-en'Provence, 1989.

Réau, Louis, *L'Europe française au Siècle des Lumières*, Paris, 1958, republished 1971.

Revolution in Fashion, European Clothing 1715–1815, Kyoto, Costume Institute, 1989. French translation, *La Mode en France 1715-1815, de Louis* XV *à Napoléon* Ier, 1990.

Ribeiro, Aileen, *Dress in Eighteenth-Century Europe 1715–1789* London, 1984.

—— *The Art of Dress, Fashion in England and France 1750–1820*, New Haven and London, 1995.

Roche, Daniel, *La Culture des apparences. Une histoire du vêtement* XVIIe*–*XVIIIe siècle, Paris, 1989.

—— 'Noblesse urbaines et vêtements dans la France du XVIIIe siècle', *L'Ethnographie*, 1984, pp. 323–31.

—— 'L'Economie des garde-robes à Paris de Louis XIV à Louis XVI', *Communication*, 'Parure, Pudeur, Etiquette', 1987, no. 46, pp. 93-117.

Rococo Costumes and Textiles; Eighteenth Century, Los Angeles County Museum of Art, November 1960–February 1961.

Ruppert, Jacques, *Le Costume*, periods: Louis XIX-Louis XV; Louis XVI–Revolution, Paris, 1931. Republished 1973–1975; with additional visual material 1990.

Ruppert, J., Delpierre, M., Davray-Piekolek, R., Gorguet-Ballasteros P., *Le Costume français*, Paris, 1996.

Tétart-Vittu, Françoise, 1780–1804 or twenty years of 'revolution amongst French heads', *Modes et Révolutions*, Musée Galliera, Paris, 1989, pp. 41–57.

Commerce, Diffusion of Fashion and the Fashion Trade

Langlade, Emile, *La Marchande de modes de Marie-Antoinette, Rose Bertin*, Paris, 1911.

Nouvion, Pierre de, and Liez, Emile, *Mademoiselle Bertin*, Paris, 1911.

Reiset, Comte de, *Modes et usages au temps de Marie-Antoinette, livre-journal de madame Eloffe marchande de modes ordinaire de la reine et des dames de sa cour.* vol I: 1787–1790, vol II: 1790–1793, Paris, 1885.

Uniforms, Official Dress and Costumes for Special Occasions

Devocelle, Jean-Marc, 'D'un costume politique à une politique du costume', *Modes et Révolutions*, Paris, Musée de la Mode et du Costume, Palais Galliera, 1989.

Jullien, Adolphe, *Le Costume au théâtre au XVIIIe siècle*, 1880.

Kahane, Martine, *Opéra côté costume*, Paris, 1995.

Lenk, Torsten, *Nationella Dräkten*, Stockholm, 1951.

Nuitter, Charles, *Costumes de l'Opéra, XVIIe-XVIIIe siècles*, Paris, 1885.

Swain, M.H., 'Nightgowns into Dressing-Gown. A Study of Men's Nightgowns in the Eighteenth Century', *Costume, the Journal of the Costume Society*, no. 6, London, 1972, pp. 10–21.

Trichet, Louis, *Le Costume du Clergé*, Paris, 1986.

Uniformes civils français, cérémonial, circonstances, 1750–1980. Musée de la Mode et du Costume, Paris, Palais Galliera, December 1982–April 1983.

Vanier, Henriette, 'Les costumes de l'ordre du Saint-Esprit. A propos d'un manteau de chevalier conservé au musée du Costume', *Bulletin du Musée Carnavalet*, no. 1. 1972, pp. 2–12.

Textiles

Abegg, Margaret, *A Propos Patterns for Embroidery Lace and Woven Textiles*, Berne, 1978

Anquetil, Jacques, *La Soie en occident*, Paris, 1995.

Arizzoli-Clementel, Pierre, *Gilets brodés. Modèles du XVIIIe siècle*. Musée des tissus: Lyon, Réunion des musées nationaux, 1993.

Bredif, Josette, *Toiles de Jouy*, Paris, 1989.

Broderie au passé et au présent, Paris, Musée des Arts décoratifs, 28 April–18 July 1977.

Chassagne, Serge, *La Manufacture de Tournemine-les-Angers*, 1752–1821, Paris, 1971.

Deguillaume, Marie-Pierre, *Secrets d'impression, carnets du textile*, Jouy, Paris, 1994.

Delpierre, Madeleine 'Un Album de modèles pour broderies de gilets', *Bulletin du Musée Carnavalet*, November 1956, pp. 2–11.

Dentelles et broderies dans la mode française du XVIe au XXe siècle, Paris, Musée de la Mode et du Costume, December 1964–April 1965. Text by M. Delpierre.

Gruber, Alain, *Ancien Régime-Premier Empire, 1785–1805 L'Art textile et la toilette*; Riggisberg, Fondation Abegg, April–November 1989.

Hartkamp-Jonxis, Ebeltje, *Sits Oost-West Relaties in Textiel*, Zwolle, 1987.

Irwin, John and Brett, Katharine B., *Origins of Chintz*, London 1970.

Lemire, Beverley, *The British Cotton Industry and Domestic market, Trade and Fashion in an Early Industrial Society, 1750–1800*, Oxford, 1984.

Les Indiennes du Val de Loire, Angers, Bourges, Orléans, Angers, Musée des Beaux-Arts, 1991–January 1992.

Buss, Chiara, *The Meandering Pattern in Brocaded Silks 1745–1775, Exhibit from the Ermenegildo Zegna Historic Textile Collection*, Milan, 1990.

Les Motifs à dentelles au XVIIIe siècle, Riggisberg, Fondation Abegg, May–October 1979.

Levey, Santina M., *Lace, a History*, Victoria and Albert Museum, London 1983.

Reddy, W. M., *The Rise of Market, the Textile Trade and French Society 1750–1900*, Cambridge, 1977.

Rothstein, Nathalie, *Silk Design of the Eighteenth Century*, Victoria and Albert Museum, London, 1990.

The Victoria and Albert Museum's Textile Collection: Woven Textile Design in Britain to 1750, New York, London 1994.

Soierie tourangelle et costumes du XVIIIe siècle . Musée des Beaux-Arts, Tours, 1972.

Soieries de Lyon. Commandes royales au XVIIIe siècle (1730–1800). Musée historique des tissus, Lyon, December 1988-March 1989.

Stavenow-Hidemark, Elisabet, *18th-Century Textiles, the Anders Berch Collection at the Nordiska Museet*, Stockholm, 1990.

Thornton, Peter, *Baroque and Rococo Silks*, 1965.

Vrignaud, Gilbert, *Vêture et parure en France au dix-huitième siècle*, Paris, 1995 (Textiles within the jurisdiction of Barrois and Lorraine, Archives de Meurthe et Moselle.)

Weigert, Roger-Armand, *Les plus beaux spécimens de la collection Richelieu*, Fribourg, 1964.

Fashion in the Press and in Illustration

Buijnsters-Smets, L., 'Kabinet van mode en Smaak' (1791–1794) 'Het Nederlandse modetijdschrift met gekleurde Haten', *Antiek*, Lochem, vol. 17, no. 9, April 1983, pp. 461–78.

Cornu, Paul, 'Essais bibliographiques sur les recueils de mode au XVIIIe siècle et au début du XIXe siècle', *Documents pour l'histoire du costume de Louis XV à Louis XVIII*, edited by Gaston Schefer, Paris, 1911.

Selected issues of *La Galerie des modes et costumes français, 1778–1787*, with table and introduction, Paris, 1912.

Dictionnaire des journaux, 1600–1789, edited by Jean Sgard, 2 vols, Voltaire Foundation, Oxford, 1991.

Gaudriault, Raymond, *Répertoire de la gravure de mode française des origins à 1815*, Paris, 1988.

Ghering van Ierlant, M.A., 'Anglo-French Fashion, 1786. The Fashionable Magazine and the Magasin des modes nouvelles françaises et anglaises 1786–1789', *Costume, the Journal of the Costume Society*, no. 17, London, 1983, pp. 64–77.

—— 'Copies des gravures de modes françaises et anglaises dans les périodiques de modes italiens 1785–1795', *Rassegna di studi e di notizie*, no. 13, Milan, 1986, pp. 335–58.

—— *Journal des Luxus und der moden*, Asgewählt und erläutert von Christina Kröll, Dortmund, 1979.

Kleinert, Annemarie, 'La naissance d'une presse de mode la veille de la Révolution et l'essor du genre au XIXe siècle', *Le Journalisme d'Ancien Régime*, Lyon, Presses Universitaires de Lyon, 1982, pp. 189–97.

—— 'La Mode, miroir de la Révolution française', *Modes et Révolutions*, Paris, Musée de la Mode et du Costume, Palais Galliera, 1989, pp. 59-81.

Rimbault, Caroline, La Presse féminine de langue française au XVIIIe siècle, Paris, typewritten thesis. 1981.

Savigny de Moncorps, Vicomte de, *Almanachs illustrés du XVIIIe siècle*, Paris, 1909.

Tétart-Vittu, Françoise, 'La Gallerie des modes et costumes français', Bibliothèque nationale, Paris, *Nouvelles de l'estampe*, no. 91, March 1987, pp. 16–21.

—— 'Presse et diffusion des modes françaises', *Modes et révolutions*, Musée de la Mode et du Costume, Palais Galliera, Paris, 1989, pp. 129–36.

—— 'Des Menus Plaisirs au studio de couture', *Le Dessin sous toutes ses coutures. Croquis, illustrations, modèles, 1760–1994*. Musée de la Mode et du Costume, Paris, Palais Galliera, 1995. pp. 25–39.

In recent years the number of university studies on the subject of costume, the clothing trade and textile manufacture has greatly increased. The notes of D. Roche's book, *La Culture des apparences*, 1989, are worth consulting for a list of theses and dissertations written under his direction. I should like to thank Madame Pascale Gorguet-Ballesteros, who is in charge of eighteenth-century costume at the Musée de la Mode et du Costume, Palais Galliera for her invaluable information about the textile bibliography. (F.T.V.)

Glossary

Bas de robe: the train fixed to the waistline of the skirt of a formal court dress.
Blonde: fine silk bobbin lace.
Brocade: silk with brocaded designs in silver and gold thread.

Caleche: women's hood supported by hoops like the hood of a coach, designed to protect high hair-styles.
Camisole: derived from *camisa*, shirt worn either in the day time or at night, later, by extension, a short jacket worn in the morning.
Caraco: jacket with basques. A *caraco à la française* had two box pleats at the back, the *caraco à l'anglaise* was boned. Before becoming a *spencer* it was named a *juste* in about 1785, then a *pierrot* or *coureur* in about 1792. By that stage the basques had become very small and were attached only at the back.
Carmagnole: short sailors' jacket worn by the *sans-culottes*.
Casaquin: waist-length *robe volante*, which produced a short jacket, fitted at the waist and reaching the hips; an ancestor of the *caraco*.
Catogan: (from Lord Cadogan): hair tied in a pigtail with a ribbon or lace; the hair was sometimes knotted.
Chemise: (see *robe*). Gown worn by both men and women.
Chenille: silk velvet braid. *En chenille* described a simple outfit worn by men in the mornings.
Circassienne: (see *robe*).
Clabaud: (see *hat*).
Clocks: patterns used as ornament on the sides of socks or stockings.
Cockade: ribbon knot fixed on to the hat or hair, worn during the Revolution by members of both sexes.
Comperes: a fake *gilet*, made of two small panels stitched to the edges of the bodice of the *robe à l'anglaise*.
Considerations: (see *paniers*).
Contouche: Polish caftan.
Coqueluchon: hood attached to the *mantelet*.
Cornette: female headdress.
Corset: lightly boned bodice.
Cravat: woman's scarf made of ruffled lace, trimmed with braid, ribbons etc.
Criarde: thick cotton underskirt, forerunner of the *panier*.

Damask: silk fabric with patterns in two matching colours.
Deshabille: informal wear for either men or women. Although it never referred to ceremonial costume, it could be used to designate elegant clothing.

DOMINO: loose cloak with a mask for the upper part of the face, worn to conceal identity, especially at masquerades.

ENGAGEANTES: lace sleeves consisting of several layers of flounces.

FURBELOWS: fabric, gathered or pleated, used to trim sleeves and skirts.
FRAC: men's coat in the English style, informal, loose-fitting and without buttons or pockets.

GAULLE: a kind of chemise.
GILET: (see *waistcoat*)

HABIT: outfit for men or women. The *habit à la française* was a men's suit consisting of three pieces (coat, waistcoat and breeches) made of the same fabric and bearing the same trimmings. After 1780 the waistcoat was usually either white or embroidered. The ceremonial outfit worn at court or for important ceremonial occasions of an order of chivalry was known as the *grand habit*, by contrast with the *petit habit*, worn for less solemn occasions. For women, the *grand habit* included a skirt over a large *panier*, a *bas de robe* (train attached at the waist), a whaleboned bodice and sleeves with lace flounces, known as *petits bonshommes*.
HAT: *à l'androsmane*, men's hat with upturned brim, *en clabaud*, *à la jacquet*, the tall hat worn by English coachmen. *A la prussienne*, a large two-cornered hat.

JACQUET or JOCKEY (see *hat*): hat worn by men and women for riding.
JUSTE: (see *caraco*).

LEVITE: (see *robe*).

MANCHETTES: lace or net half-sleeves worn under the sleeves of a woman's dress.
MANTELET: small cape covering the shoulders, usually with hood attached.
MITTENS: gloves with half fingers, or with just the thumb.

PALATINE: fur stole, made fashionable by the Princess Palatine.
PANIERS: underskirts stretched over metal hoops. The *panier à guéridon* was round, the *panier à coudes* oval. Short, rigid and light, the *panier jansénsite* and the *considération* supported dresses without the need for heavy petticoats.
PIERROT: (see *caraco*).

REDINGOTE: heavy overcoat with lapels for riding or travelling. The man's *redingote* was adapted for women, becoming a dress that opened to reveal a skirt and waistcoat.
ROBE: female gown covering the whole body, opening in front to show the petticoat. Under the Regency the *robe ballante* or *robe volante* was in fashion, with sleeves *en pagode* and the bodice open in front; this was worn over a *panier*. This style was replaced by the *robe à la française* in the middle of the century, then by the *robe à l'anglaise*, which had a whaleboned back. The *robe à la polonaise*, with its sleeves *en sabot*, was often worn with a waistcoat underneath. Three draped panels which could be raised by cords (like curtains) formed loops over the underskirt. Another version of the *robe à la polonaise* sported short sleeves over the long sleeves of the underdress and was

called the *robe à la circassienne*. The *robe à la turque* had funnel-shaped sleeves, a turned-over collar, a gathered bodice and a draped sash tied on one side. The *lévite* was a long loose gown with a girdle knotted around the waist. The *robe en chemise* was a light tunic with gathered bodice, or with a low neckline, belted at the waist. The *robe fourreau* (sheath) was worn by children; made in one piece, it fastened at the back. The over-dress, *robe de dessus*, or mantle was worn over a skirt called a *jupon*. The *jupon* was called a *tablier* (apron) if it covered only the front; it could be seen through the opening in the coat.

RUCHE: tightly pleated lace gauze.

SACK: the English version of the *robe française*.

SIMARRE: magistrate's robe.

SLEEVES: a fitted sleeve finishing in a point on the top of the hand was called a sleeve *en amadis*; a sleeve with a very wide, tight cuff on a man's coat was called *en pagode*; on a woman's gown, however, the sleeve *en pagode* was funnel-shaped and opened on to layers of flounces. (The flounces were called *en raquette* when they were made of flat pleats). The sleeve *en sabots* was to be found only on the *robe polonaise*; it had gathered bands around the cuff and reached to only just below the elbow.

SOUTANE: priest's gown; the *soutanelle* was a short version.

STOMACHER: triangle of fabric pinned to the bodice.

THERESE: large gauze hood worn to protect an elaborate hair-style.

TOQUET: women's bonnet; or a cap worn by a child.

WAISTCOAT: (veste) worn under the man's jacket, and could have sleeves of plain fabric. The basques gradually disappeared. After about 1780 the *veste* became known as a *gilet*. In 1789 this was straight at the waist and had lapels. A *jaquette* was a short waistcoat worn for hunting or in the country, in imitation of the sleeved jackets worn by peasants.

WHALEBONED BODICE: the ancestor of the *corset*; it was a very tight bodice stiffened with whalebones.

WIG: false hair, called a *perruque* in French. The *perruque à marteaux* had several pigtails; the *perruque en ailes de pigeon* had rolled curls on either side of the face.

ZOUPANE: long-sleeved gown, Turkish in origin, worn in Poland.

SSCCA 391
.0094
4
D363